ALEXANDER THE GREAT

Selections from Arrian

TRANSLATIONS FROM GREEK AND ROMAN AUTHORS

TRANSLATIONS FROM GREEK AND ROMAN AUTHORS

Series Editor: GRAHAM TINGAY

Alexander the Great

Selections from Arrian

J. G. LLOYD
Head of Classics
St Lawrence College, Ramsgate

CAMBRIDGE UNIVERSITY PRESS

Cambridge
London   New York   New Rochelle
Melbourne   Sydney

Published by the Press Syndicate of the University of Cambridge
The Pitt Building, Trumpington Street, Cambridge CB2 1RP
32 East 57th Street, New York, NY 10022, USA
296 Beaconsfield Parade, Middle Park, Melbourne 3206, Australia

First published 1981

Printed in Great Britain by Redwood Burn Limited
Trowbridge, Wiltshire

Library of Congress catalogue card number: 81–9453

British Library cataloguing in publication data
Arrian
Life of Alexander the Great. – (Translations from
Greek and Roman authors)
1. Greek prose literature – Translations into
English
I. Title   II. Lloyd, J.G.
III. Series
888'.01'08   PA3255

ISBN 0 521 28195 4

The cover illustration is part of a large mosaic from Pompeii
depicting the battle of Issus. The mosaic is a copy of an older
Greek painting and this detail shows Alexander on his horse,
eager for victory. It is reproduced by courtesy of the Mansell
Collection.

Contents

Alexander's route

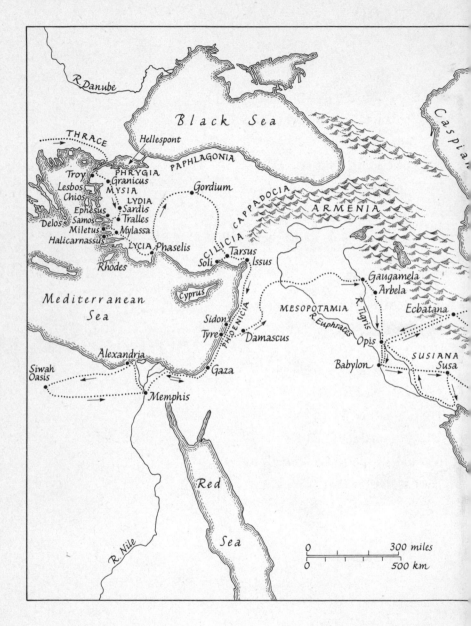

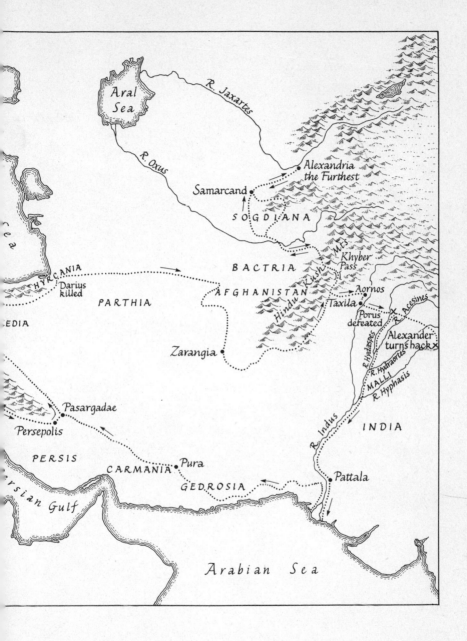

Aral
Sea

R. Jaxartes

R. Oxus

Samarcand

Alexandria
the Furthest

SOGDIANA

HYRCANIA

Darius
killed

PARTHIA

Zarangia

BACTRIA

AFGHANISTAN

Hindu Kush

Khyber
Pass

Aornos

Taxila

Porus
defeated

R. Acesines

Alexander
turns back

R. Hydaspes

R. Hydraotes

MALLI

R. Hyphasis

EDIA

Pasargadae

Persepolis

PERSIS

CARMANIA

Pura

GEDROSIA

R. Indus

INDIA

Pattala

Persian Gulf

Arabian Sea

Greece

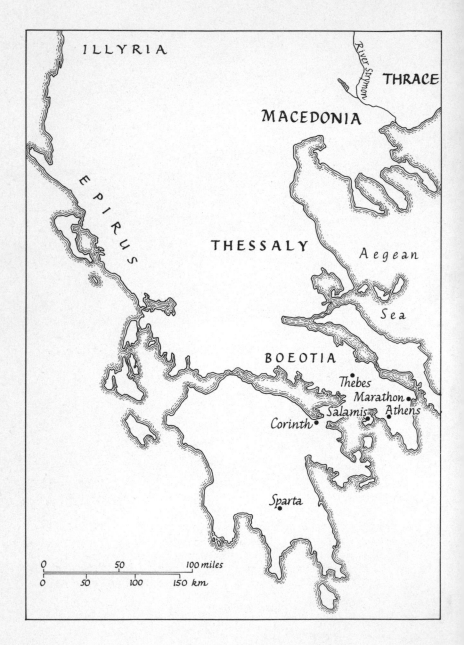

1   Introduction

In 336 B.C. a young man, aged only twenty, succeeded to the throne of Macedonia on the murder of his father. It was a dangerous throne indeed. His claim to it was likely to be challenged; an attempt on his life was a distinct possibility. Subject peoples to north and south saw this as the perfect moment to rebel. No normal man could have hoped to deal with such problems.

Nearly thirteen years later this same young man, still not thirty-three years old, died at Babylon, in the heart of the Persian empire. Not only had he overcome his difficulties at home, defeated neighbouring tribes, and established himself as the acknowledged leader of his people; even the hosts of Persia had fallen before him in a series of mighty battles, Egypt had accepted his rule, and he had led his armies to India and the very edge of the known world. By the time they turned back his men had covered over eleven thousand miles in eight years, for most of them a journey accomplished every inch on foot. The empire now covered something like two million square miles. You have only to read of the battles, the sieges – especially of Tyre and Aornos – and marches such as the crossing of the Gedrosian Desert, to wonder what sort of men could achieve such things. But the men were normal enough. It was their leader, Alexander, who was unique. Here was a personality to make the difficult easy and the impossible possible.

This book may seem to be a military account, but first and foremost it is the story of a man. It sets out to show what Alexander was like; brave to the point of rashness, passionate to the point of murder, a military genius, administrator and empire builder, but above all an inspiring leader of men. We must begin by examining his background.

Macedonia
If you were to study British history of the sixteenth century you would gain a vivid impression of the Elizabethan age. You would read of Drake, Raleigh and Shakespeare, the defeat of the Spanish armada, the elegant life of Elizabeth's court. But it would be clear to you that London and the south were the focus of all that mattered. What you heard of Scotland to the north would leave you with the impression of a less civilised race, disorganised in its feuding tribes and hostile to the more advanced nation to the south. Of course this would be shamefully unfair to the Scots. But the same is true for those who study the history of Greece. Everything seems to centre on Athens; Sparta is treated with

some respect; Corinth and Thebes have their place; but Macedonia is a barbarous land to the north. Yet if we allow ourselves to move on from the fifth century B.C., certainly the golden age of Greek achievement in the arts, to the following century, when so much seems to have fallen into decay, we find one of the most remarkable men of all time, Alexander the Great. And he was a Macedonian.

Macedonia lies at the very north of Greece, cut off from its richer southern neighbours by mountainous country. Communication to the south was by narrow passes, easily blocked. The Macedonians probably came into contact more often with the peoples of southern Europe, modern Yugoslavia and Bulgaria, than with other Greeks. Whether one thought of them as Greek or barbarian depended on one's prejudices. They spoke Greek, with a strong dialect of their own, so that a conversation between an Athenian and a Macedonian would have been like a Londoner talking to a highland Scot. But the Macedonians themselves considered that they were Greek, and it was on this basis that Alexander's father, Philip, established himself, not as the conqueror of Greece but as its leader. In the same belief Alexander took over his father's mantle as the leader of the Greek nation against the barbarian Persians. Macedonian kings did their best to establish contact with the recognised values of Greece. Greek artists and poets were always welcome at the Macedonian court, and the playwright Euripides left Athens in his old age to live out the rest of his life there. When Philip wanted a tutor for his son he invited from Athens the distinguished scholar Aristotle. One of the most important items on the young prince's syllabus was to be the poems of Homer. The religious bond with the rest of Greece was equally strong. Macedonian kings claimed descent from Heracles, and thus also from Zeus; the worship of Dionysus was popular, and Alexander's mother in particular was an active devotee.

In one respect, however, Macedonian development had fallen behind most of the rest of Greece – it was still ruled by kings. The country was a loose amalgamation of tribes, with flexible boundaries as fringe areas broke away, or renewed their loyalty. In such circumstances there was little chance of making democracy work. Government needed a strong leader who could unite the different sections of the country by his own personality, supported by judicious political marriages. It was all a normal king could do to hold his country together, maintain his own position, and ward off his enemies to the north. It needed an extraordinary man to make Macedonia a match for other nations, and doubtless that is why Macedonia's greatness coincides with the rule of two extraordinary men, Philip and Alexander. The target of their ambitions was Persia.

Greece and Persia

In the late sixth century B.C the expanding power of Persia came into conflict with the Greeks, whose settlements fringed the coast of Asia

Minor. Persian expansion and Greek resistance created a series of wars culminating in Alexander's 'final solution', the total conquest of the Persian empire. The great stories of the Persian invasion of mainland Greece in the fifth century B.C. are well known; the glorious Athenian victory at Marathon, still remembered by the event held in the Olympic Games and at other athletics meetings, the heroic self-sacrifice of the three hundred Spartans at Thermopylae, Themistocles' cunning which led the Persian fleet into a trap at Salamis. But it is all too easy to think that that is the end of the story. Far from it: the existence of the Athenian empire stemmed from the ideal of uniting the Greeks to resist the Persians, and for a while that is what they did. When Sparta found herself at the head of Greek affairs, after winning her great war with Athens, she accepted her responsibility towards the Greeks of Asia Minor, after some dithering, and Spartan troops operated on Persian soil in the 390s. It was instinctive for Greeks to feel that Persia was the enemy. To a man who wished to establish leadership in Greece a clear way to unite the country behind him, and to divert the cities from quarrels with each other, was to organise a war against Persia.

When Philip secured the throne of Macedonia, acting first in 359 B.C. as regent for his infant nephew, but soon accepted as king in his own right, he spent over twenty years expanding his power throughout Greece. By diplomacy and by conquest he built up the kingdom until in 338 B.C. he defeated the combined forces of his enemies at Chaeronea in Boeotia. Philip used his victory to convene a meeting of the Greek states, which only Sparta (of any consequence) boycotted, and at its first full meeting in the summer of 337 B.C. war was declared on Persia, Philip being formally appointed commander-in-chief. The expressed reason was to take vengeance for the Persian destruction of Greek temples during their invasion nearly one hundred and fifty years earlier. Such was the length of Greek memories, such the depth of feeling against Persia.

Philip immediately began his preparations, and an advance force was sent into Asia Minor to establish a base on Persian soil. His murder a year later, before he himself could join his army, could have put an end to the whole enterprise. But his son was a man of even greater drive and ambition.

The Young Alexander

Alexander was born in 356 B.C., when Philip was still struggling to establish himself on the throne of Macedonia and to make his country a force to be reckoned with. His mother Olympias was a princess of the neighbouring kingdom of Epirus, and by all accounts a woman of passion and great personality. Alexander was educated in every way as befitted a future king; the learned Aristotle was his tutor, and his wide interests are demonstrated by the inclusion of historians, artists and scientists of all sorts in the circle of men closest to him during his conquests. Alexander did not merely wish to conquer, but also to understand and record what he found. Obviously he was outstanding in the arts of war, and his skilful horsemanship is attested by his successfully riding Bucephalas, a horse which no one else could manage, when still little more than a child. Bucephalas remained his favourite horse and accompanied him as far as India.

Alexander's first taste of authority came when he was only sixteen. His father, absent from the capital on a campaign, entrusted the Royal Seal to his son, in effect leaving him to act as regent. A Thracian tribe at once revolted and Alexander led out his army to conquer them. He re-settled their captured capital, naming it Alexandropolis after himself. Two years later he led a crucial cavalry charge at the great battle of Chaeronea, which finally established Philip's authority over Greece.

But despite this, in a country such as Macedonia, Alexander could not take it for granted that he would succeed to the throne. Marriage was a matter of political policy; kings took various wives; a son might succeed because of the status of his mother rather than on his own merits. In 337 B.C. Philip took a new wife of full Macedonian blood. Olympias returned home to Epirus, and Alexander quarrelled with his father to the extent of having to leave the country. Although there was a reconciliation, the new queen duly produced a son, and no one could guarantee that Alexander would ever ascend the throne, especially if Philip lived until the new prince grew up. And so it is natural that when Philip was murdered, at his daughter's wedding to Olympias' brother, fingers should point, some at Olympias, some at Alexander. The assassin was a member of Philip's bodyguard, and he was overpowered and killed on the spot, so that no one can show whose agent he was, if anyone's. Certainly a case that could not be proved then cannot be proved now. What is certain is that Alexander was able to secure the throne, Olympias returned to Macedonia and was highly influential in the running of the country, especially during Alexander's subsequent absence in Asia. Of course the new-born prince was 'disposed of' soon to be followed by his mother (roasted alive by Olympias, if we believe one highly coloured, if unlikely, version), and various other relations who may have been dangerous. In no other way could Alexander secure his throne, and ruthlessness had to be a fact of his life.

Outside the country drastic action was equally necessary. The southern Greeks, led by Thebes and Athens, planned to break free of Macedonian domination. Alexander at once headed south. As with so many talented generals speed of movement was one of his outstanding characteristics. Another was his remarkable way of dealing with natural barriers. He avoided the blockade of a pass into Thessaly by cutting steps over Mount Ossa, and his sudden appearance in their midst persuaded his enemies to instant repentance. The Greek alliance formed by

Philip was renewed and Alexander accepted as its lawful leader. He could now turn against his northern neighbours, and a fierce campaign in Thrace and Illyria both reduced the rebels to submission and showed the energy and imagination of this remarkable young man. Unfortunately a rumour reached Greece that he had been killed, and rebellion flared up again, especially in Thebes. If Alexander were to be free to march against Persia his enemies at home had to be crushed once and for all. Within a fortnight he was before the walls of Thebes. This time there was no surrender by the defenders, offers of terms were scornfully refused. The assault was fierce and decisive. The city of Thebes was razed to the ground and those who had survived the fighting, thirty thousand according to some possibly exaggerated versions, were sold into slavery, man, woman and child. Small wonder that Greece cringed before the conqueror. He could turn to the great enterprise of the Persian campaign without any fear of further risings behind him.

Alexander's Army

The Macedonian army as created by Philip and developed by Alexander was probably the finest fighting force of ancient times. The hard core of any Greek army was its infantry phalanx, which normally formed the centre of the line. In Alexander's army this was a force of nine thousand men, sometimes called the *Infantry Companions*, divided up into six battalions. These men were heavily armed, and their special weapon was the pike, a thrusting-spear about fourteen feet long. In solid formation they must have looked invulnerable, and indeed unapproachable. However their manoeuvrability was rather limited and their main value was in a set battle. They were supported, and often outshone, by the *Guards*, three battalions each a thousand strong, including the *Elite Corps* later known as the *Silver Shields*. These were more lightly armed than the Infantry Companions and so more versatile in the varying needs of Alexander's campaign. Accordingly they appear far more often in the story. The infantry force was completed by detachments from Alexander's Greek allies and his northern neighbours, of whom only the Agrianians deserve special mention. They figure prominently in almost every action Alexander ever took, especially when speed was essential, and one cannot help but compare their role with that of the Gurkhas of the British army.

In ancient Greek warfare cavalrymen were rarely prominent, but in the open lands of Persia they were vital, and Alexander based much of his success upon them. The *Cavalry Companions*, about two thousand strong, were a crack force, showing a vitality and dash which regularly threw their enemies into confusion, leaving them ready to be mopped up by the infantry. A similar number of cavalrymen came from Thessaley, an area noted for its cavalry, while the Paeonians and Thracians also provided cavalry units which we often find mentioned.

It is clear too that although we know less about them the engineers

5

and support units of the army were of equally high quality. Their siege and assault equipment was very advanced; for instance their catapults could propel an eight pound missile up to four hundred and fifty yards, and greater weights a proportionately shorter distance. We have only to read of the remarkable siege operations at Tyre, or the ascent of the Rock of Aornos, to see that this army was much more than a body of soldiers. They were men who could accomplish feats which hardly bear thinking of today, and through it all shines the inspiring leadership of a man whose personal example and military genius welded them into the incomparable force which they proved themselves to be.

Arrian's History

We shall follow Alexander's story as Arrian recorded it. Arrian was born over four hundred years after the death of Alexander. Although a Greek, he served in the Roman army gaining useful military experience, and governed one of Rome's eastern provinces in territory which had been part of Alexander's empire. But his life's work was the writing of his account of Alexander's campaigns. Obviously the value of his work depends on his sources of information. In Arrian's times several eye-witness accounts existed, written by men who had taken part in the campaigns. Arrian refers frequently to two officers in Alexander's army, Aristoboulus and Ptolemaeus, who subsequently became king of Egypt. Both published their memoirs after Alexander's death, which in Arrian's view made them more likely to be truthful, as they had nothing to gain by flattery of their hero. We may more cynically wonder whether they perhaps could still gain by exaggerating their own parts, praising their friends and criticising their enemies. Their views of the court disputes and scandals can hardly have been impartial. But their evidence must be as good as we can ever hope for, and Arrian seems to have used them thoughtfully and to have compared them carefully.

Another account written at the time was that of Callisthenes who went as official historian to Alexander's expedition. He was an outspoken character and was eventually executed for treason, but what was published can only have been what Alexander was prepared to approve, and was essentially a propaganda document for Greek consumption. Nearchus, Alexander's admiral, was another who published an account after Alexander's death, and Arrian seems to have consulted it for the latter part of his work. In the section dealing with Alexander's death, Arrian also refers to the Royal Diaries. The authenticity of this document, which only seems to have survived in a fragmentary state, is much disputed. A popular theory is that it was eventually published to refute the rumour that Alexander had been poisoned, by giving a detailed account of his last days. We cannot really be sure about the value of any of these accounts, but we can feel confident that Arrian has done his best with the material at his disposal.

It was also inevitable in ancient times that legends should attach themselves to great men. Alexander himself, anxious to support claims of divine descent, was only too ready to encourage such stories, and after his death no doubt all sorts of exaggerated tales became widespread. Arrian would see no reason to doubt many of them, for the mythology which Alexander took for granted was a natural part of Arrian's outlook as well. We can only use our common sense in assessing what we read. But this book presents the story as Arrian told it.

2 Conquest of Asia Minor

As soon as his authority was firmly established in Greece Alexander set out on his grand expedition, in May of 334 B.C. He cannot have foreseen how remarkable it would become, and yet his ambition was clear in his first acts. He began by sacrificing to Protesilaus, traditionally the first Greek to land in Asia on the expedition against Troy some 750 years earlier. He then saw to it that he was himself the first to land on this occasion. He visited the site of Troy and sacrificed at the tomb of Achilles, greatest of all the Greek heroes, whose example he proposed to follow. At the temple of Athene he dedicated his own armour, receiving in return a shield and weapons said to date back to the Trojan War. We know the value of propaganda nowadays; so did Alexander.

Meanwhile his army too had crossed to Asia and was ready to seek out the enemy. The Persians only had their locally based forces, with Memnon, the commander of their fleet, advising them. They toyed with adopting a scorched-earth policy while they fell back to join Darius, their king. But they did not yet see why they should go onto the defensive against an invader of their country, and so they decided to give battle. The line of the river Granicus seemed to offer an ideal position, and here we shall take up the story with Arrian. Notice Alexander's personal example – not to mention how close he came to death, and so the ruin of everything, in the very first encounter – and see how skilfully he conducted events after the battle, and used his booty, to strengthen his bond with the army, and so to achieve a propaganda as well as a military success.

Alexander was now advancing towards the river Granicus with his army in battle formation. He had drawn up the heavy infantry in a doubled phalanx, posted the cavalry on the wings, and ordered the baggage columns to follow on behind. To scout out the enemy position Hegelochus was leading a party consisting of the cavalry lancers and about five hundred light infantry. Alexander was not far from the Granicus when riders from the scouting party galloped up at full speed to report that the Persians were drawn up for battle on the far bank of the river. Alexander began at once to make his arrangements to give battle, but Parmenio came to him and put the following argument:

'Your majesty, in the present situation I really think it is best to encamp as we are, on the river bank. I do not believe that the enemy, with far fewer infantry than ours, will dare to pitch camp near to us, and so it will be possible for our army to cross easily at dawn. We shall be across before they can get back into position. But as it is I do not think we can attempt action without risk, because we cannot take the army across the river on a broad front. We can see that there are many deep pools, while the banks themselves are very high and in some places quite sheer. We will scramble out of the river in disorder and in column, which is the weakest formation; the enemy cavalry, drawn up in massed formation, will then fall upon us. A failure in our first action will at once have serious consequences, and will put at risk the result of the whole war.'

Alexander replied, 'I know that, Parmenio. But I would be ashamed if I could cross the Hellespont easily and then found that this little stream' (that was the scornful way he spoke of the Granicus) 'could prevent us from crossing just as we are. I do not agree that this is right for the reputation of the Macedonians, and it does not fit in with the way I usually react when I meet danger. I think the Persians will gain in confidence and believe themselves to be as good fighters as the Macedonians if they manage to avoid suffering the sort of disaster which they are now afraid of.'

So saying he sent off Parmenio to take command of the left wing, and himself moved over to the right. Philotas, Parmenio's son, had been put in command of the extreme right, with the Cavalry Companions, the archers and the Agrianian spearmen. Posted along with him was Amyntas the son of Arrabaeus, with the cavalry lancers, the Paeonians and Socrates' squadron. Next came the Guards under Parmenio's son Nicanor, and then the companies of Perdiccas the son of Orontes, Coenus the son of Polemocrates, Craterus the son of another man called Alexander, Amyntas the son of Andromenes and Philip the son of Amyntas. On the extreme left were posted the Thessalian cavalry under Calas the son of Harpalus, with the allied cavalry next under Philip the son of Menelaus and then the Thracians commanded by Agathon. After them came the infantry, the companies of Craterus, Meleager and Philip, extending to the centre of the whole line.

The Persian cavalry numbered about twenty thousand, and they had almost as many foreign mercenaries serving on foot. They had formed up their cavalry extending along the river bank

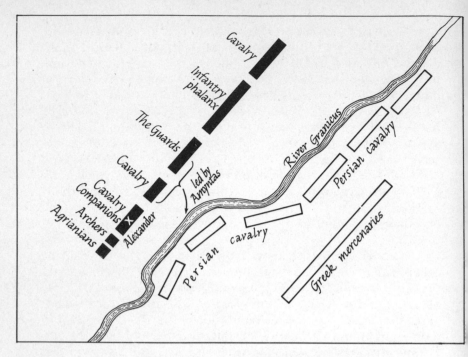

The battle at the river Granicus

in a long, solid line, while the infantry were behind the cavalry. The ground stretching back from the bank rose steeply. Where they could see Alexander himself (and he was clearly identifiable by the splendour of his armour and the close attentions of those around him) facing their left wing, they had massed their cavalry squadrons more closely on the bank.

For a while the two armies stood on the river bank, shrinking from what was to come, and there was deep silence on both sides. The Persians were waiting for the Macedonians to begin the crossing, so that they could attack them as they reached dry land. But Alexander leapt on to his horse and called to his bodyguard to follow him and to show what they were made of. He ordered Amyntas son of Arrabaeus to advance into the river with the scout cavalry, the Paeonians and one company of infantry. In front of them he sent Ptolemaeus the son of a man called Philip with Socrates' squadron, which happened to be the leading cavalry squadron on that day. He himself advanced into the river leading the right wing, to the blast of trumpets and with war cries raised to the God of Battle. He kept his troops at an angle to the current so that the Persians could not attack him from the flank as he landed, and so that he himself could come to grips with them in the closest possible formation.

Where the troops with Amyntas and Socrates were the first to reach the bank, the Persians shot down onto them from above, some throwing javelins into the river from the full height of the bank, others coming down onto the lower ground by the water's edge. Then there was a hand-to-hand cavalry struggle as the one side tried to get clear of the water and the others tried to stop them; there were constant volleys of Persian javelins, while the Macedonians fought back with thrusting-spears. But the Macedonians, heavily outnumbered, suffered badly in their first attack; their footing was insecure and they were fighting from a lower position in the river, while the Persians had the height of the bank in their favour, and in particular they had the pick of their cavalry posted at this point, Memnon's sons and Memnon himself facing the danger with them. The first of the Macedonians who came to grips with them were cut down, despite their bravery, except for those who fell back to Alexander as he approached. For he himself was now almost there, leading the right wing; and indeed he was the first to charge the Persians at the point where the whole mass of their cavalry and the officers as well were posted. Around him a fierce struggle developed, while rank after rank of Macedonians were now crossing without difficulty. Although the battle was fought on horseback it was more like an infantry battle. Horse pushed against horse and man grappled with man, the Macedonians struggling to drive the Persians once and for all from the river bank onto level ground, the Persians to stop the enemy getting clear of the water and to drive them back into the river. But already Alexander's men were getting the upper hand, through their strength and experience, and because they were using lances of cornel wood against short javelins.

At that moment Alexander's spear was broken in the battle. He called to Aretis, one of the royal grooms, for another spear, but he also was struggling with a broken spear and fighting bravely with the stump. He showed it to Alexander and told him to ask someone else. Demaratus, a Corinthian and one of Alexander's bodyguard, gave him his own spear, which Alexander seized; then seeing Mithridates, Darius' son-in-law, riding well ahead of the others, leading a detachment of cavalry in wedge formation, he also galloped forward in front of his companions, struck

Mithridates in the face with his spear and knocked him off his horse. At that Rhoisaces charged Alexander and struck him on the head with his curved sword; this cut off part of the helmet, which nevertheless checked the blow. But Alexander struck him down, driving his spear through his breast-plate into his chest. Spithridates had actually raised his sword to strike Alexander from behind, but Cleitus the son of Dropides anticipated him, struck him through the shoulder of his sword arm and cut it off. Meanwhile those of the cavalry who were managing to get clear of the river continued to join the group with Alexander.

The Persians were now under pressure from all sides; men and horses were being struck in the face with spears, they were driven back by the cavalry and suffered a great deal of harm from the lightly armed troops who had mingled with the cavalry. They cracked first at the point where Alexander was leading the attack. But once their centre had given way both wings of the cavalry also broke, and there was a total rout. About a thousand of the Persian cavalry died, but the pursuit was not pressed because Alexander turned against the foreign mercenaries. Their massed ranks remained where they had first been posted, more in dismay at the unexpected result of the battle than from any firm decision. Alexander advanced his phalanx against them and ordered the cavalry to attack from all sides. Thus he soon surrounded and slaughtered them, and none escaped unless any were unnoticed among the corpses, but about two thousand were taken alive...

On the Macedonian side about twenty-five of the Companions died in the first attack. Bronze statues of them were set up at Dium, made on Alexander's orders by Lysippus, who was also chosen to make a statue of Alexander. Of the other cavalry more than sixty died, and about thirty infantry. On the following day Alexander had them buried with their weapons and other equipment. He gave to their parents and children exemption from local taxes and from all other personal obligations and property taxes. He also showed great concern for the wounded. He himself visited each one, looked at their wounds asking how they had suffered them, and even allowed them to exaggerate the story as they told it. He had the Persian officers buried, and the Greek mercenaries who had died fighting on the side of the enemy. But those whom he had taken prisoner he bound in chains and sent to hard labour in Macedonia because, although they were Greeks, they had fought on the side of foreigners against Greece, quite contrary to normal Greek sentiment. He sent to Athens three hundred suits of

12

Persian armour as an offering to the goddess Athene, and he ordered this inscription to be engraved there: 'Alexander, son of Philip, and the Greeks except the Spartans give these offerings taken from the foreigners who live in Asia'.

From this triumph Alexander made straight for Sardis, the main Persian city in Asia Minor, which immediately surrendered to him. At once he made his purpose clear; he had come as a liberator, not a conqueror. There would be no destruction, taxation would be at the existing level, Greek cities which accepted him would be given democratic governments. On that basis Ephesus admitted him, but Miletus, hearing of an enormous Persian fleet in the vicinity, decided to resist. In such situations the wisest move is to be on the winning side; but the Milesians were backing the wrong horse. Alexander's smaller fleet secured the harbour first and held its mouth. The Persian fleet, cut off from a land base and essential supplies, especially of drinking water, could not operate effectively. Using siege methods which we shall read of fully at Halicarnassus and Tyre, Alexander compelled the city to surrender. Despite its resistance he gave Miletus a democracy and then headed south into Caria where more vigorous opposition could be expected. A striking feature of Alexander's conquests is his skill in assaulting walled cities, and the first detailed account we read tells of his capture of Halicarnassus in Caria.

Alexander then set out for Caria because he had been told that a considerable force of Persians and foreign mercenaries had gathered in Halicarnassus. On his march he captured all the cities between Miletus and Halicarnassus and then camped near the city, over half a mile away, ready for a long siege. Geographically the place was very strong, and any weak spot which could be detected had been reinforced well in advance by Memnon personally; for he had been chosen by Darius as governor of southern Asia Minor and commander of the whole fleet. Many soldiers and foreign mercenaries had been left in the city, and many of the Persians as well. The warships were anchored in the harbour so that there was also plenty of help from the sailors.

On the first day Alexander led a force up to the wall by the Mylasa Gate, and there was a counter-attack from the city, while missiles were also aimed at him from long range. Alexander's men retaliated and easily drove the enemy back, blockading them in the city. A few days later Alexander took the Guards, the mounted Companions, and the infantry regiments of Amyntas, Perdiccas and Meleager, with the archers and Agrianians, and

13

went round the city to the side facing Myndus. He wanted to reconnoitre the wall to see if it was more vulnerable there, and if he could capture Myndus by a surprise attack. For if Myndus fell into his hands it would be a great help in the siege of Halicarnassus. He had also had an offer of surrender from the people of Myndus if he came quietly in the night. Thus as agreed he approached the wall about midnight. But there was no sign of surrender, and his siege engines and ladders were not with him, because he had not come prepared for a siege but expecting the surrender of the city. Nevertheless he moved the Macedonian phalanx up to the wall and gave orders to undermine it. The Macedonians demolished one tower, but its fall did not leave the wall defenceless. The citizens resisted vigorously and many reinforcements, arriving by sea from Halicarnassus, made further progress and the capture of Myndus by immediate attack impossible. So Alexander withdrew without achieving his objective and again turned his attention to the siege of Halicarnassus.

First he filled in the moat which had been dug in front of the city, forty-five feet wide and twenty-two feet deep. This would make it easy to bring up the towers, from which he intended to bombard the defenders of the wall, and the other siege engines to batter down the wall itself. The moat was easily filled in and the towers brought up, but the Halicarnassians made an attack in the night, intending to burn the towers and the other engines which had been brought forward or were not far away but ready to be moved up. However they were easily driven back again behind their walls by the Macedonian sentries and by those who were roused by the disturbance and came to the rescue. A hundred and seventy of them were killed, including Neoptolemus the son of Arrabaeus and brother of Amyntas, who had deserted with some others to Darius. Sixteen of Alexander's soldiers died, but about three hundred were wounded, because, as the attack had taken place at night, they had been less well armed for protection against wounds.

A few days later two Macedonian infantrymen of Perdiccas' company, who shared a tent and were drinking together, were boasting about themselves and the splendid things they had done. Their spirit of competition grew, and the wine roused their feelings still more, so that they armed themselves and attacked the wall at the high point facing Mylasa. They simply wanted to show off and not really to run the risk of fighting the enemy. But some of those in the city saw the pair foolishly approaching the wall and charged out at them. They killed the two, who had now come too close, and showered spears on the more distant soldiers; they had the advantage in numbers and the difficult ground in their favour, because they were charging and throwing their missiles from a high point. At this, some others from Perdiccas' force rushed out, and the Halicarnassians too, so that a violent struggle developed by the wall. Those who had rushed out were again driven inside the gates by the Macedonians, and in fact the city was all but captured. For the walls were not well guarded at that moment, and as two towers and the wall between them had collapsed there would have been an easy entrance for the army if they had all tackled it. The third tower too had been weakened and would have been easily demolished if they had undermined it. But before the Macedonians could take advantage of it the defenders built a semicircular wall of brick to replace the collapsed wall on the inside, which they had no difficulty in doing because of the numbers working on the building.

On the next day Alexander brought up his siege engines at this point and again there was an attack from the city aimed at burning them. Part of the protective fencing near the wall and one of the wooden towers was burnt, but the men with Philotas and Hellanicus, who had been put on guard duty there, successfully defended the rest. When Alexander appeared during this attack the raiders threw away their firebrands, and many threw down their weapons as well, as they fell back behind the wall. Yet at first the defenders had the better of it through the advantage of their position on higher ground. They not only aimed their missiles straight ahead at the soldiers advancing in front of the siege engines, but they also fired from the flanks from the towers which still stood on each side of the breach in the wall, and were almost able to aim at the rear of the attackers as they came up to the new replacement wall.

A few days later, Alexander again brought up his siege engines to the newly built inner brick wall and took personal charge of the operation. There was a counter-attack in full force from the city, both by the breach in the wall where Alexander himself was, and by the Triple Gate, which was not at all what the Macedonians had expected. Some threw firebrands and whatever else could help to set the siege engines on fire. But Alexander's men reacted vigorously; big stones were hurled by catapults from the siege towers and javelins were showered onto the enemy, so that they were easily routed and fled back into the city. At this point the slaughter was considerable as the townsfolk had attacked in greater numbers and with greater daring. Some were killed in hand-to-hand fighting with the Macedonians, others near the collapsed wall where the passage was too narrow for their number and the rubble of the wall was difficult to scramble over.

The enemy force which came from the Triple Gate was met by Ptolemaeus, the commander of Alexander's bodyguard, who took with him the companies of Addaeus and Timander and some of the lightly armed troops. They routed the townsfolk without difficulty, who had the further misfortune that a narrow bridge built over the moat collapsed under their weight in the retreat. Many fell into the moat, some were trampled to death by their own side, others were shot from above by the Macedonians. But the greatest slaughter actually took place around the gates, because they were shut in a panic before they should have been, as the defenders were afraid that the Macedonians might get in along with the fugitives. Many of their own side were shut out and the Macedonians killed them by the walls. In fact the city was all but captured, and would have been if Alexander had not recalled his army, because he wanted to save Halicarnassus if some sign of goodwill should be offered by its people. About a thousand of the citizens had been killed and about forty of Alexander's soldiers, including Ptolemaeus the commander of the king's bodyguard, Clearchus the commander of the archers, and Addaeus a battalion commander, as well as other distinguished Macedonians.

The Persian officers Orontobates and Memnon now met and agreed that in the present circumstances they could no longer resist the siege. They saw that part of the wall had already collapsed, part was badly weakened, many of the soldiers had been killed in their counter-attacks, and others were disabled by wounds. Realising this, at the second watch of the night, they set light to the wooden tower, which they had themselves built to combat the enemy siege engines, and to their weapon stores. They also set fire to the houses near the wall, and the fire spread to others from the armouries and the tower, burning fiercely as the wind spread it. Some of the Persians withdrew to Arconessus, others to the height called Salmakis. When the news was brought to Alexander by some who had deserted at this act, and he had himself seen the extent of the fire, even though it was all happening about midnight he led out the Macedonians and killed those who were still setting fire to the city. He gave orders to save any Halicarnassians who were found in the houses.

Dawn was now breaking. Alexander saw the heights which the Persians and mercenaries had occupied but decided not to besiege them. He thought it would be a serious waste of time because of the nature of the ground, and it was not very important to him now that he had captured the city. He buried those who had been killed in the night, ordered the soldiers in charge of the siege engines to take them to Tralles, and razed the city to the ground.

Alexander was now anxious to secure the country further south, and to continue to deprive the enemy fleet of possible bases. Although winter was approaching he pressed on along the coast. However he sent Parmenio to spend the winter in Sardis with most of the transport and cavalry, for whom winter operations in rough country were inappropriate. He also showed another touch of genius in man-management by sending home those of his troops who were most recently married. They could spend the winter with their wives and return in the spring, accompanied, it was hoped, by further recruits.

However we must not assume that Alexander was universally popular. His story is dotted with reports of plots against him. The details are usually obscure, as they would be since plotters are not in the habit of letting everyone see what they have in mind, and stories of curious and unlikely omens are often added. Arrian records the first such plot as happening in this winter. He never tells us the ultimate fate of the plotter, but from other sources we hear that he was executed three years later at the time of the alleged plot of Philotas, of which we shall read in its proper sequence.

While Alexander was still at Phaselis he was told that another man called Alexander, the son of Aeropus, was plotting against him. He was one of the Companions and at that time commander of the Thessalian cavalry. This Alexander was a brother of Heromenes and Arrabaeus, who had been involved in the murder of Philip, but although he was implicated the king had let him go because he had been among the first of his friends to side with him when Philip died, and he had armed himself and accompanied the new king to the palace. Later he kept him with him in a position of honour, making him general in Thrace, and he had later appointed him to command the Thessalian cavalry when Calas, the previous commander, was sent to take charge of a province.

The details of the plot were revealed as follows. Amyntas deserted to Darius and took with him a message and a letter from this Alexander. Darius therefore sent Sisines, a reliable Persian from his court, to the coast supposedly to visit Atizues, the governor of Phrygia, but really to meet this Alexander, and to promise to make him king of Macedonia, if he killed the king, and to give him a thousand talents of gold as well. But Sisines was caught by Parmenio, and he told him why he had been sent. Parmenio therefore sent him under guard to Alexander, who also got the same story out of him. He called his friends together and they discussed what should be done about the traitor. The Companions felt that the king had made a mistake previously in giving the best of the cavalry to an unreliable man, and that now he must get rid of him as quickly as he could before he became too friendly with his Thessalians and organised a rebellion with their help.

A sign from the gods also worried them. For while Alexander had still been besieging Halicarnassus and was taking a rest at mid-day, a swallow had flown above his head twittering loudly, and settled here and there on the bed, making an unusually troubled noise. Alexander was too tired to be woken up, but disturbed by the sound he gently brushed the swallow away with his hand. But although he touched it it was by no means frightened into flying away, but actually settled on his head and did not go away until Alexander was fully roused. Alexander took the swallow's behaviour seriously and told Aristander of Telmissus, a man who interpreted omens. Aristander told him that a plot by one of his friends was meant, but it also indicated that the plot would be discovered. For the swallow is a domestic bird, friendly to man, and more of a chatterer than any other bird.

Putting this together with the story of the Persian, he sent Amphoterus, the brother of Craterus, to Parmenio. He also sent some Pergaean guides to show him the way. Amphoterus wore native clothing, so as not to be recognised on the journey, and reached Parmenio undetected. He took no written message from the king, for it seemed unwise to put anything in writing in such an affair. But he gave his message verbally as instructed, and so the other Alexander was arrested and held under guard.

> In the spring of 333 B.C. the Macedonian forces re-assembled at Gordium, and here one of the best-known incidents in Alexander's story occurred. In itself it may not be important, but it should be seen in the light of Alexander's constant concern for good propaganda. Of course the cutting of the Gordian knot has also become proverbial in our own language.

When Alexander reached Gordium he was anxious to go to the

citadel, where the palace of Gordius and his son Midas stood, to see the waggon of Gordius and the knot of the waggon yoke. There was a story about the waggon, widespread among the local people, telling that Gordius was a poor man of the ancient Phrygians who had a small plot of land to cultivate and two pairs of oxen. They say that he used one pair to plough and the other to pull his waggon. Once when he was ploughing an eagle settled on the yoke and stayed there until sunset. Gordius was amazed at the sight and went to consult the Telmissian fortune-tellers about the omen; for the Telmissians are clever at explaining divine signs, and all of them, men, women and children inherit this gift. When he approached a Telmissian village he met a girl drawing water and told her about the eagle's behaviour. The girl, who was descended from a prophetic family, told him to go back to the same place and sacrifice to Zeus the King. Gordius asked her to go with him and help with the sacrifice, and he sacrificed as she told him. He then married the girl and they had a son called Midas.

When Midas had grown to be a fine, handsome man the Phrygians were involved in a civil war, and they had a prophecy that a waggon would bring them a king who would stop the war. When they were actually discussing this, Midas arrived with his father and mother and came to a stop in his waggon at the meeting place. Recognising the prophecy the Phrygians decided that this was the man whom the god had prophesied that the waggon would bring. They made Midas king, he put an end to the civil war, and on the citadel he offered his father's waggon in thanks to Zeus the King for sending the eagle.

Another story told about the waggon was that whoever undid the knot of the waggon yoke should rule Asia. The knot was made of the bark of a cornel tree and neither the beginning nor the end of it could be seen. Alexander could not find a way to untie the knot, but did not want to leave it fastened in case this caused any disturbance among the common people. Some say that he hacked at the knot with his sword and cut it through, claiming to have undone it. Aristoboulus says that he took out the pin from the pole, which was a peg driven right through the pole, holding the knot, and so pulled the yoke from the pole. I cannot confirm how Alexander dealt with the knot, but he and his companions left the waggon sure that the forecast about the undoing of the knot had been fulfilled. That night also thunder and lightning gave a further sign, and so the next day Alexander sacrificed to the gods

19

who had given the sign and had confirmed that he had undone the knot.

In the summer Alexander headed back to the coast, without meeting serious opposition, but at Tarsus he fell ill. Alexander's relationship with his men is always fascinating, perhaps the best measure of his real worth. As we have seen there were plots against him, but the story of his cure at Tarsus shows a confidence which can only have inspired his loyal followers.

At Tarsus Alexander fell ill. Aristoboulus says that fatigue was the cause, but others record that it was because he dived into the river Cydnus and had a swim when he was hot and sweating, as he was eager for a bathe. The Cydnus flows through the middle of the city, but as its source is in the Taurus mountains and it flows through open country its water is cold and clear. Alexander was seized by cramp and violent fevers, and could not sleep. The other doctors thought he would die, but Philip, an Acarnanian doctor who attended Alexander and was very highly regarded for his medical skill, and not without reputation as a soldier, wanted to treat him with a particular medicine, and Alexander told him to do so. While Philip was preparing the cup a letter was given to Alexander from Parmenio, telling him to be on his guard against Philip; for he had heard that he had been bribed to poison Alexander. The king was reading the letter, and still had it in his hand, when he took the cup in which the medicine was. He gave the letter to Philip to read, and while Philip was reading Parmenio's warning Alexander drank the medicine. Philip at once made it clear that the medicine was all right; for he was not dismayed by the letter but simply told Alexander to follow his further instructions; if he did he would recover. Alexander was indeed cured and his illness passed, while he had also proved to Philip that he was his faithful friend and to the rest of his attendants that he was firm in his confidence in them and was undismayed in the face of death.

Alexander's illness at Tarsus had been a serious delay. The Persians had at last organised themselves, under King Darius personally, to face the invaders on the field of battle. On the other hand, as Alexander did not appear, Darius lost his patience and headed north to find him, as the next portion from Arrian relates. At the same moment Alexander at last received news of the whereabouts of Darius' army. This was the occasion for one of his flashes of remarkable energy, and in his determination to catch the Persians off guard he led his army along the coast road at an astonishing pace. Passing through Issus, where he left the sick and wounded, he covered about seventy miles in two days. Yet unknown to him Darius was moving north by an inland route, and the armies must have passed each other separated only by a mountain ridge. When Darius decided to cross the ridge he was doubtless amazed, but equally delighted, to find himself in Alexander's rear. Alexander's communications were cut, his army was tired, the initiative seemed lost. On the other hand Darius was now in confined country, circumstances better suited to Alexander if a set battle were to be fought. Characteristically, Alexander decided on immediate action.

Meanwhile Darius was waiting with his army. He had chosen a plain in Assyria, open in every direction and suitable for the enormous size of his army and convenient for cavalry manoeuvres. Amyntas the son of Antiochus and a deserter from Alexander had advised him not to leave this spot, for plenty of space favoured Persian numbers and equipment. So Darius waited. But Alexander had a long delay in Tarsus because of his illness, and again in Soli where he held a sacrifice and parade of the army, and finally when he made a campaign against the hill tribes of Cilicia. This upset Darius' plan. He always turned gladly to whatever opinion was the most pleasing, and under the influence of flatterers, whose company is bad for kings and always will be, he was convinced that Alexander no longer planned to advance. In fact he believed that Alexander was hesitating because he knew that he himself was approaching. Various advisers encouraged him, telling him that he would trample down the Macedonian army with his cavalry. Amyntas insisted that Alexander would come wherever he learnt Darius to be, and urged him to wait there. But the worse advice convinced him, because at that moment it was more pleasant to hear. Moreover some supernatural influence was leading him to a place where his cavalry would be of no benefit nor would the number of his men and missiles, and where he could not show off the splendour of his army. In fact he was about to give an easy victory to Alexander and his troops. For it was fated that the Persians should lose their rule of Asia to the Macedonians, just as the Medes had lost it to the Persians, and the Assyrians to the Medes before that.

Darius now crossed the mountain ridge through what are called the Amanian Gates, and advanced to Issus. He arrived undetected behind Alexander. After occupying Issus he cruelly tortured and killed all the Macedonians who had been left there because of illness. On the next day he advanced to the river Pinarus. When Alexander heard that Darius was behind him he thought the report incredible, but he sent some of the Companions back to Issus in a thirty-oared ship to see if the news was true. The party on the ship discovered quite easily that the Persians were camping there because the sea forms a bay at this point, and they reported back to Alexander that Darius was indeed nearby.

> Alexander delivered a speech of encouragement to his men, secured the mountain pass in the night, and advanced towards Darius' position next morning, fanning out into battle formation as the ground became more open. His left flank stretched to the sea and his right to the hilly country inland.

When the troops were formed up Alexander led them on for a while with occasional halts, so that his advance seemed quite leisurely. Darius did not lead his troops forwards once they were in formation, but stayed on the river banks, which were steep in many places, and at some points where his position seemed more open to attack he built a stockade. By this he at once revealed to Alexander's men his cowardly character. When the two armies were close together Alexander rode all along the line calling on his men to show their courage. He called upon the senior officers of course, addressing them by their names and proper titles, but also spoke to the squadron and company commanders and any of the mercenaries who were well known for their high quality or for any act of courage. And from all sides there arose a shout not to delay but to charge the enemy.

Alexander was still leading them on in formation, slowly at first, although he now had Darius' army in full view, so that no part of the phalanx would get out of line in a too rapid advance. But when they were in missile range Alexander's own troops, with himself in command of the right wing, were the first to dash into the river. He wanted to dismay the Persians by the speed of the charge, and to suffer least harm from their archers by coming to grips quickly.

It worked out as Alexander had guessed; for as soon as hand-to-hand fighting developed those on the left wing of the Persian army were routed. At that point Alexander and his own force scored a brilliant victory. But the Greek mercenaries on Darius' side attacked the Macedonians at a point where they saw their phalanx seriously disrupted. For while Alexander, charging

22

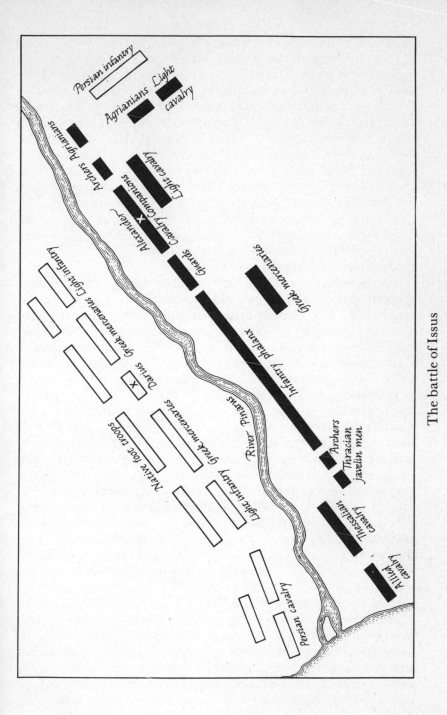

The battle of Issus

eagerly into the river and coming to grips with the enemy, had already driven back the Persians set against him, the Macedonians in the centre had not gone into action with equal speed. As they found the banks steep at many points they had been unable to keep their front in line, and here their phalanx had split, breaking away towards the right. There the struggle was fierce, as the Greek mercenaries tried to force the Macedonians back into the river and to save the day for those who were already in flight, while the Macedonians did not want to fall short of the success which they could see Alexander had already gained, nor to lose the reputation of the phalanx, until then known as unconquerable. There was also the influence of racial prejudice between the Greeks and Macedonians. At that point Ptolemaeus the son of Seleucus, a brave soldier, died along with a hundred and twenty-one other distinguished Macedonians.

But then the units on the right wing, as they saw the Persians opposite them in retreat, wheeled round against Darius' foreign mercenaries and towards their own struggling comrades. They drove the enemy back from the river, and when they overlapped the shattered wing of the Persian army they launched a flank attack on the mercenaries and began to cut them down. Meanwhile the Persian cavalry facing the Thessalians did not remain on their own side of the river when the action began, but charged across and launched a vigorous attack on the Thessalian squadrons. At this point the cavalry battle was desperate, and the Persians did not waver until they realised that Darius was in flight and that their own mercenaries had been cut off and massacred by the phalanx. Then indeed flight was open and complete. The Persian horses suffered badly in the retreat, for their riders were heavily armoured, while the cavalrymen who were retreating in great numbers along narrow tracks, in fear and disorder, came to as much harm by being trampled by each other as they did from the enemy pursuit. The Thessalians pressed them hard, so that there was as much killing of the cavalry as of the infantry in the rout.

As soon as Darius' left wing had been thrown into a panic by Alexander and he saw it cut off from the rest of the army, Darius was one of the first to flee in his chariot, just as he was. While he found level going for his escape he sought safety in his chariot. But when he came to ravines and other obstacles he abandoned the vehicle and stripped off his shield and cloak; he even left his bow in his chariot. He mounted his horse and fled, and only night, which soon fell, saved him from being caught by Alexander. As long as there was light Alexander pursued at full speed, but when it grew dark and he could not see the ground in front of his feet he turned back towards the camp. But he took Darius' chariot, and his shield, cloak and bow as well. His pursuit had in fact been too slow because when the phalanx first broke he had wheeled round, and he had not taken up the chase personally until he saw the foreign mercenaries and Persian cavalry driven back from the river.

On the Persian side Arsames, Rheomithres and Atizues, men who had served as cavalry officers at the Granicus, died. Sabaces the governor of Egypt, and Boubaces were other distinguished Persians to die. Of the others about a hundred thousand fell, and over ten thousand cavalry among them, so that Ptolemaeus the son of Lagus, who was with Alexander in the pursuit, claims that when the pursuers of Darius came to a ravine they crossed it on the bodies of the dead.

Darius' camp was at once stormed and captured, and his mother and wife, who was also his sister, and his infant son were taken. Two of his daughters and a few other noble Persian ladies attending them also became prisoners. But the other Persians had sent their womenfolk to Damascus, with the rest of their baggage, while Darius had sent there most of his money and other things which go with a great king, even on a campaign, to satisfy his extravagant living. So no more than three thousand talents were captured in the camp. But not long afterwards the money at Damascus was captured by Parmenio, who was sent to seize it. This then was the outcome of the battle fought in the archonship of Nicocrates at Athens in the month of November [333 B.C.].

Although Alexander had himself been wounded in the thigh by a sword he visited the wounded on the next day. He had the bodies of the dead collected and gave them a splendid funeral, with the whole army drawn up in battle formation in its finest display. He delivered a speech in praise of all whom he himself had seen or had heard by agreed report to have done any outstanding deed in the battle, and he honoured each as he deserved by a gift of money . . .

Nor did he neglect Darius' mother, wife or children. Some who have written the history of Alexander say that on the night when he returned from his pursuit of Darius and went into Darius' tent, which had been set aside for him, he heard the wailing of women and similar sounds not far away. He asked who the women were and why they were in a tent so near his. Someone said, 'Sir, Darius' mother, wife and children have been told that you have his bow and royal cloak, and that his shield has also been brought back. They are weeping at his death.' At this Alexander sent Leonnatus, one of the Companions, to tell them that Darius was alive; he had abandoned his weapons and cloak in his chariot as he fled and this was all that Alexander had. Leonnatus went to the tent and gave them the news about Darius. He added that Alexander would allow them to live in royal state in every way and to retain their royal titles. His war with Darius was not fought out of personal enmity, but he had made legitimate war for rule over Asia.

Ptolemaeus and Aristoboulus tell this story, but there is another version, that on the following day Alexander visited them personally, accompanied only by Hephaestion. Darius' mother did not know which was the king, for both were dressed in the same way, and so she went towards Hephaestion and bowed down to him because he looked the taller. Hephaestion stepped back and one of the queen's attendants pointed to Alexander and told her that he was the king. She shrank back, embarrassed by her mistake, but Alexander said that she had not made a mistake, for Hephaestion was an Alexander too. I have recorded this although I do not know whether it is true or entirely false. But if it happened I can only praise Alexander for his sympathetic behaviour towards the ladies, and for the trust and honour he showed towards his friend. On the other hand, if the historians felt that Alexander would have acted and spoken like that, I can again only praise him for it.

3 Phoenicia, Egypt, and Darius' defeat

Of course the victory at Issus was spoiled by the escape of Darius, but its biggest bonus was that it finally secured Asia Minor. Those people who had expected Alexander to lose as soon as he met the full might of Persia, and so had not whole-heartedly supported him, hastily changed their ideas. With an active fleet operating on the coast the Persians had always been able to threaten Alexander's communications and supplies. Now their fleet found the coastal people less welcoming; they could no longer freely recruit crews, obtain supplies, and carry out repairs. In particular Darius was no longer able to send them essential financial support. One further push from Alexander could put the Persian fleet out of the war for ever and leave him free to operate at will on the mainland. Accordingly he advanced down the Phoenician coast, and was welcomed everywhere, except at the key city of Tyre. One might have thought a siege here impossible, but nothing was beyond Alexander, and this proved to be one of his most remarkable and important successes.

Alexander easily persuaded his officers to agree to the attempt upon Tyre. He also had the support of a sign from the gods; for that very night in a dream he saw himself approaching the wall of Tyre when Heracles greeted him and led him into the city. Aristander explained it as meaning that the city would be taken, but only with great labour, because Heracles' achievements had involved labour. It was in fact obvious that the siege of Tyre was a great undertaking. For the city was an island, protected on all sides by high walls, while any action at sea clearly favoured the Tyrians in the present circumstances, because the Persians had command of the sea and the Tyrians themselves had a numerous fleet. Even so Alexander had his wish.

He decided to build a mole from the mainland to the city. There is a shallow channel there, the water near the mainland consisting of muddy shoals while the deepest part of the crossing, near the city, is about eighteen feet deep. There was an abundance of stones, and plenty of wood which they heaped on top of the stones. It was easy to drive stakes into the mud, which itself

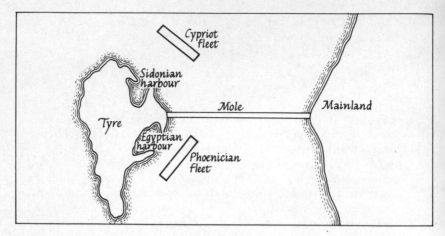

The siege of Tyre

also acted as a binding for the stones to keep them in place. The Macedonians were very enthusiastic about the work, as was Alexander who was himself present, explaining everything, praising and rewarding with gifts of money those who did anything particularly well. While they were working on the mainland end of the mole they made good progress as they were building in shallow water with no opposition. But when they came to deeper water near the city they suffered severely under bombardment from the high walls. They were dressed for work rather than for fighting, and the Tyrians, who still had control of the sea, sailed up to various points on the mole in their warships and made it impossible for the Macedonians to carry on. In answer, the Macedonians set up two towers on the mole, where it had now extended well out to sea, and mounted siege engines on them. Skins and hides were used as screens to protect them against fire-arrows from the walls and to give cover from the arrows to those working there. At the same time the Tyrians who sailed up and attacked the men working on the mole could be bombarded from the towers and might easily be driven off.

The Tyrians met this with the following device. They filled a horse-transport ship with dry brushwood and other inflammable timber, set up two masts in the bows, and raised the bulwarks all round as far as they could, so that she could hold as many wood-shavings and torches as possible. In addition they loaded her with pitch, sulphur, and anything else likely to cause a great blaze. On both masts they fitted a double yard-arm and hung cauldrons from it containing anything else which would help to make the blaze flare up when it was poured or thrown onto it. They put weights in the stern to raise the bows high out of the water, then waited for a wind blowing towards the mole.

The ship was towed stern first by warships, and when they were near to the mole and the towers the Tyrians set light to the wood, towed her forward as fast as the warships could go, and grounded her on the edge of the mole. The men from the burning ship easily swam to safety. As a result an enormous blaze engulfed the towers, and when the yard-arms broke they poured onto the fire all that had been prepared to feed the flames. The men on the warships, staying in their position near the mole, poured volleys of arrows at the towers so that those who were bringing anything to fight the flames could not safely get near. At that moment, when the towers were already well alight, many Tyrians streamed from the city, boarded small boats, and landing on the mole at various points easily pulled down the palisade set up to protect it. They also burnt all the siege engines which the fire from the ship had not caught.

Alexander ordered his men to begin the mole again from the mainland end, building it broader so that it would hold more towers, and told the engineers to construct fresh siege engines. While this was in progress he himself took the Guards and the Agrianians and went to Sidon to collect all the warships which he had there, as the siege seemed likely to be more difficult while the Tyrians remained in control of the sea.

> From various sources Alexander obtained over two hundred ships, and four thousand Greek mercenaries also arrived at this time to fight with him.

When his fleet was organised he put as many of the Guards as he thought he needed for the action on the decks, assuming that the battle would not be a matter of manoeuvres so much as of hand-to-hand fighting. He then set out from Sidon and sailed to Tyre with his ships in close formation. He was himself on the right wing, which was farther out to sea. With him were the Cypriot kings and all the Phoenicians except Pnytagoras, who along with Craterus was directing the left wing of the whole fleet. Previously the Tyrians had decided to fight at sea if Alexander sailed against them, but now they saw a totally unexpected number of ships. For they had not yet heard that all the Cypriot and Phoenician ships were with Alexander. At the same time the attackers were advancing in close formation. At first Alexander's ships had lain-to at sea before approaching the town, but when the enemy did not put out against them they advanced at full speed in battle order. When the Tyrians saw this they decided not to give battle; instead they blocked the harbour mouths with as many warships as there was room for, and kept guard so that the enemy fleet could not anchor in any of the harbours.

When the Tyrians refused battle Alexander sailed up to the city. He decided not to try to force an entrance into the harbour facing Sidon because of the narrowness of its mouth, and because he could see that it was blocked by many warships lying bows-on. However the Phoenician ships made a head-on attack on the three warships moored furthest out and sank them; the crews easily swam away to the friendly shore. Alexander's fleet then moored near the new mole by the shore where there seemed to be shelter from the wind. On the next day Alexander ordered the Cypriots and their admiral Andromachus to blockade the city off the harbour facing Sidon, and the Phoenicians on the other side of the mole by the harbour facing Egypt, where his own quarters were.

By now many engineers had been collected from Cyprus and all over Phoenicia, and many siege engines had been built, some on the mole, some on the horse-transport ships which Alexander had brought from Sidon, some on the slower of the warships. When everything was ready they brought up the siege engines along the mole, and others on the ships which were moored at various points along the wall, and began a direct assault.

The Tyrians had placed wooden towers to fight from on the battlements facing the mole, while at any other point where siege engines were brought up they defended themselves with missiles and bombarded the ships with fire arrows, so that they terrified the Macedonians from approaching the wall. Opposite the mole the wall was about a hundred and fifty feet high and correspondingly thick, built of large blocks of stone set in mortar. The Macedonian horse-transports and warships which were bringing the siege engines up to the wall did not find it easy to approach the city at this point, because many boulders had been thrown into the sea, which hindered their advance. Alexander decided to haul these out of the water, but the work was difficult as it had to be done from ships and not from dry land. In particular the Tyrians reinforced some of their ships, drove them against the anchors of the warships, and by cutting the cables made it impossible for their opponents' vessels to anchor close in. Alexander similarly reinforced a number of thirty-oared boats and placed them broadside on in front of the anchors so that enemy attacks were blocked by them. Even so divers went down and cut the cables. In answer the Macedonians used chain for their anchors instead of rope and the divers could do nothing further about it. Eventually the Macedonians fastened ropes from the mole to the boulders and hauled them up out of the water. Then using their siege engines they disposed of them in deep water where they were no longer likely to do any harm. When the approach to the wall had been cleared of obstacles the ships easily sailed close in there too.

The Tyrians were now in difficulties at every point and decided to make an attack on the Cypriot ships which were on guard off the harbour which faced Sidon. Some time before, they had fitted sails across the harbour mouth so that the manning of warships could not be seen. At about midday, when the soldiers were scattered about their duties and Alexander had just left the fleet at the other side of the city to go to his quarters, they manned three quinqueremes and quadriremes and seven triremes, with their best crews, and stationed the best armed marines with the greatest confidence in sea-fighting to fight on deck. At first they sailed out in single file, rowing silently without any calling of orders. But when they were turning towards the Cypriot ships and were about to come into sight, with a mighty shout and mutual encouragement they charged, keeping perfect time with the oars.

On that particular day it happened that Alexander had gone to his tent, but had not taken his usual rest and had quickly returned to the fleet. The Tyrians attacked the moored ships unexpectedly and found some absolutely empty, while others were being manned with difficulty by anyone who happened to be there when the noise of the attack was heard. So in the first charge they at once sank the quinquereme of King Pnytagoras and the ships of Androcles of Amathus and Pasicrates of Thurieus. The others they drove aground and broke up.

But when Alexander heard of the attack of the Tyrian warships he ordered the majority of the ships with him to take up position, as each was manned, at the mouth of the Egyptian Harbour, so that no other Tyrian ships could venture out. He himself took his quinqueremes and the five triremes which had been manned the most quickly, and sailed round the city against the Tyrians who were already out. The defenders on the wall saw the enemy approach and Alexander himself on board. They shouted to their crews to go about, and as their cries were inaudible in the noise of the action they used various signals to indicate that they should turn back. But the sailors noticed Alexander's approach too late. When they did they turned at once and fled for the harbour, and a few of them succeeded in getting away, but Alexander's squadron caught most of them. Some were put out of action, while a quinquereme and a quadrireme were captured right by the harbour entrance. Those on board suffered little loss of life, for when they realised that their ships were trapped they easily managed to swim back into the harbour.

The Tyrians now had no further prospect of help from their ships, and the Macedonians began to bring their siege engines up to the wall. Those that were brought via the mole did nothing worth mentioning because of the strength of the wall. Ships carrying siege engines were also brought up to the side of the city facing Sidon, but as there was no progress here either Alexander turned his attention to the wall on the south side, facing Egypt, probing at every point. The wall was first seriously shaken there and a part was actually broken down. Alexander went so far as to throw gangways across to the breach in an exploratory attack, but the Tyrians easily beat him off.

Three days later, after waiting for a calm and making a speech of encouragement to his officers, Alexander again brought his sea-borne engines up to the city. First he battered down a considerable part of the wall, and when the gap seemed wide enough he ordered the assault ships to withdraw. He then brought up two others carrying gangways, which he planned to throw across to the breach in the wall. The Guards manned one ship under the command of Admetus, while Coenus' company of Infantry Companions manned the other. Alexander was himself with the Guards, ready to mount the wall as soon as it became possible. He ordered some of the warships to sail round to the two harbours, in the hope that they could force the entrance while the Tyrians were concentrating on the assaulting troops. Other ships carrying the missiles for the siege engines or with archers on their decks he ordered to circle the wall, putting in wherever possible, and to lie within range if it were impossible to close right in, so that the Tyrians could be bombarded from all sides and would be in an impossible position.

When the ships with Alexander reached the wall and the gangways were thrown up from them, the Guards resolutely forced their way up. Admetus showed himself a fine soldier in that action; Alexander was there too, taking a vigorous part in the fighting and keeping an eye on the others to see who performed any brilliant act of courage in the face of danger. The wall was first taken at the point where Alexander stood. The Tyrians were easily driven off it as soon as the Macedonians had a firm footing and were not facing a sheer climb. Admetus was the first to set foot on the wall, and as he urged his men on he was hit by a spear and died there. But Alexander, close behind him, held the wall with his followers. Once some towers and the sections of wall in between were in his control he made his way along the battlements towards the royal quarters, because he thought the descent into the city would be easier there.

Meanwhile the Phoenicians who had been posted in their ships off the Egyptian Harbour forced their way in, smashing through the booms, and set about the ships in the harbour. They rammed some where they were and forced others aground. The Cypriots, off the harbour facing Sidon, which did not even have a boom, sailed in and easily captured the city at that point. The main body of Tyrians abandoned the wall, when they saw it in enemy hands, but massed together at the shrine of Agenor and made a stand there. Alexander advanced against them with the Guards and killed some on the spot as they fought, while others he pressed hard as they fled. There was great slaughter, since the troops from the harbour already held the city and Coenus' company had also forced its way in. In their anger the Macedonians fell upon everything. They were enraged by the length of the siege and also because the Tyrians had earlier captured some of their men, sailing from Sidon, taken them up onto the wall so that they were visible from the camp, and had slaughtered them there and thrown them into the sea. About eight thousand Tyrians died, while on the Macedonian side Admetus, who had been the first to reach the wall, died in the assault, showing himself the gallant soldier that he was, and twenty of the Guards fell with him. In the whole siege they lost about four hundred men.

King Azemilcus, the most important of the Tyrians, and some Carthaginians who had come to their mother-city to pay honour to Heracles, according to an ancient custom, fled to the temple of Heracles. Alexander gave all these a free pardon. He sold the rest into slavery, and the number who were sold, both Tyrians and foreigners captured there, was about thirty thousand. Alexander sacrificed to Heracles and held a parade with his army in full array. The fleet also held a review in honour of Heracles, and there were athletic events and a torch-race in the temple precinct. In the temple Alexander offered the siege engine which first breached the wall, and the sacred Tyrian ship of Heracles, which he had captured in the assault, was also offered to the god.

> After Tyre, Alexander's target was Egypt, perhaps the oldest civilisation then known, and a wealthy and powerful unit in the Persian empire. Alexander also had religious reasons for visiting Egypt, as we shall see. On his route he found further resistance at Gaza, where a siege almost as difficult as the one at Tyre was necessary. However without the problem of the sea on this occasion he was able to take the city and wipe out its population in two months. In Egypt he was welcomed as a liberator, and the story goes, although Arrian does not seem to know of it, that he was actually crowned as Pharaoh in the city of Memphis. It was in Egypt that he left his most lasting memorial, the city of Alexandria. Arrian's account is brief, but includes typically symbolic detail.

From Memphis Alexander sailed down the Nile towards the sea, taking on the ships the Guards, archers, Agrianians and the Royal Squadron of Cavalry Companions. He reached Canobus and after sailing round Lake Mareotis landed where the city of Alexandria, named after him, now stands. The site appeared to him to be ideal for founding a city, and he believed that a city there would be prosperous. He was eager to push on with the work, and personally marked out the plan, showing where the market-place had to be laid out, how many temples there were to be, and the gods to whom they would be dedicated, Greek gods and the Egyptian Isis. He also marked where the city wall was to run. He made a sacrifice to initiate the work and it proved favourable.

The following story is also told, and I do not find it unlikely. Alexander wanted to leave the ground-plan of the city wall for the builders, but had nothing with which to mark the ground. One of the builders suggested collecting the barley-meal, which the soldiers carried in their packs, and sprinkling it on the ground while the king led the way. So the circle of the surrounding wall which Alexander wanted to make for the city was marked out. The interpreters of omens, and especially Aristander of Telmissus who was said to have made many other correct prophecies to Alexander, considered this and said that the city would be prosperous, and especially in the fruits of the earth.

While he was in Egypt Alexander also visited the oracle of the god Ammon at the Siwah Oasis. This visit did much to change the image which Alexander liked people to have of him. He began to let himself be thought of as the son of Ammon, whom the Greeks equated with Zeus. Remarkable and mysterious tales surrounded the visit, probably encouraged in later accounts by Ptolemaeus, one of Arrian's main sources, who became king of Egypt after Alexander's death. Alexander was always careful to observe proper religious ritual, and later he often claimed to be acting in accordance with instructions received from Ammon.

Alexander now became eager to visit Ammon in Libya. One reason was that he wanted to consult the god because the oracle of Ammon was said to be infallible. Also Perseus and Heracles had consulted it – Perseus when he was sent by Polydectes to kill the Gorgon, and Heracles when he went into Libya to find Antaeus and into Egypt to find Busiris. Alexander was eager to rival Perseus and Heracles, for he was descended from them both, and he also traced his own descent partly from Ammon, just as legends trace the descent of Heracles and Perseus from Zeus. At any rate he set off to visit Ammon with this intention, to learn more accurately about himself, or at any rate to say that he had.

He travelled along the coast as far as Paraetonium, through un-inhabited but not waterless country, for two hundred miles according to Aristoboulus. From there he turned into the interior where the oracle of Ammon was. The track is through desert, for the most part sandy and waterless. But Alexander had plenty of rain, and this was attributed to divine help. A further point was also put down to the god's help; for when the south wind blows in that area it heaps the sand up over the track and the signs of the route are hidden. Just as at sea, there is no means of knowing which way one must go over the sand, and there are no marks along the track, no hill nor tree nor mound of solid earth rising up, by which travellers can judge the route, as sailors can by the stars. Alexander's army was going off course and the guides were in doubt about the route. But Ptolemaeus the son of Lagus says that two snakes went in front of the army, making some sort of spoken sounds, and Alexander told the guides to follow them, trusting in divine help. The snakes led the way to the oracle and back again. Aristoboulus, agreeing with the commoner version of the story, says that two crows flew in front of the army and acted as guides for Alexander. I can guarantee that he had some divine help, because it is so very likely, but the different versions of the story

35

have prevented me from being sure of its exact nature.

The temple of Ammon is entirely surrounded by sandy and waterless desert. But in the centre is a small area – at its widest it amounts to about five miles – full of fruit trees, olives and date palms, and it is the only place in the surrounding country where dew falls. A spring wells up there not at all like other springs which flow from the ground. For at midday the water is cold to the taste, and it is as cold as can be to the touch. But as the sun sets towards evening the water is warmer, and from evening it grows warmer still until midnight, when it is at its warmest. From midnight onwards it cools again, and at dawn it is cold, but coolest at midday; and it changes like this regularly every day. Natural salt is also mined in this area and the priests of Ammon take some of it to Egypt. When they go to Egypt they pack it in baskets woven from palm leaves and take it as a gift to the king, or perhaps to someone else. The grains are large, some of them more than three fingers wide, and it is as clear as crystal. The Egyptians and others who are particular about religious details use it for sacrifices, because it is purer than sea salt.

Alexander viewed the site with wonder, and put his question to the god. When he had heard the answer which he wanted to hear, so he said, he travelled back to Egypt by the same route, according to Aristoboulus, but following a direct route to Memphis, according to the version of Ptolemaeus.

This visit to the Siwah Oasis had taken place early in 331 B.C. Alexander now retraced his steps to Tyre and spent three months dealing with problems of organisation before moving away from the coast into Mesopotamia. Darius was meanwhile planning for a decisive battle. He seems to have been quite content to choose his site and wait, confident that Alexander would come to face the challenge. A better general might have done more to harass Alexander's supplies or to block him at the crossing of the Tigris. But Darius was not a great general, and naturally any rational man comparing the armies would have been sure that Alexander had no chance. The victory obviously shows the fighting quality of the Macedonian army, but even more it shows the dynamic strength of Alexander's personality and will.

Darius' whole army was said to consist of forty thousand cavalry, a million infantry, two hundred scythe-chariots, and a few elephants, as the Indians from the west of the Indus had brought about fifteen of them. With this army Darius encamped at Gaugamela near the river Boumodus, about seventy-five miles from the city of Arbela, in country that was flat in every direction. For wherever the country was uneven and so unsuitable for cavalry the Persians had levelled it off, to make it convenient for chariots and horsemen. For some people had persuaded Darius that in the Battle of Issus he had been at a disadvantage because of lack of space, and he was easily convinced.

When Alexander received this news from captured Persian scouts he remained where he was for four days. He gave his army a rest after their march and strengthened the camp with a ditch and palisade. For he had decided to leave the baggage animals and those of the soldiers who were unfit for battle, and to advance into action with his combat troops carrying nothing but their weapons. Accordingly he assembled his force at night and led them out at the second watch, intending to meet the enemy at dawn. When Darius was told that Alexander was already approaching he drew up his army for battle, while Alexander similarly continued to advance in battle formation. The armies were fully seven miles apart and could not yet see each other, for there were hills lying in between them.

Alexander was less than four miles away, and his army was already coming down from the hills, when he caught sight of the enemy and halted his phalanx. Calling together the Companions, generals, cavalry commanders and senior officers of the allies and foreign mercenaries, he discussed whether he should lead the phalanx into action at once. Most of them told him to do this, while Parmenio thought it best to encamp there and to scout out the whole area, in case there was any suspicious detail or any problem such as ditches or hidden stakes fixed in the ground, and also to get a better sight of the enemy formation. Parmenio's advice was accepted and they encamped there, in the formation in which they were going to fight.

Alexander took the light-armed troops and Cavalry Companions and rode out on a complete survey of the area where the battle was likely to be fought. On his return he again called together the same officers. He said that they did not really need his encouragement to fight; they had long ago been inspired by their own courage and by their frequent glorious deeds already accomplished. But he expected each of them to encourage his own men, the company, squadron, brigade or section of the phalanx which he commanded. For in this battle they would not be fighting for Lowland Syria or Phoenicia or Egypt, as before, but for the whole of Asia, to settle at that very moment who the ruling power must be. He had no need to rouse them to brave deeds by a long speech, for courage was in their hearts from birth. But each one must be responsible personally for discipline in danger, for total silence when they had to advance quietly, for a rousing cheer when it was the moment to cheer, and for the most terrifying war-cry when it was the time to raise it. They must themselves be fully alert for their orders, and must see that the orders were passed smartly to the ranks. Each man, and the army as a whole, must remember that in his own conduct lay danger if he were slack and success if he did his duty reliably.

After these and similar brief words of encouragement Alexander was assured by his officers that he could rely on them. He then gave orders for the army to eat and rest. The story goes that Parmenio came to Alexander's tent and advised him to attack the Persians during the night; for his attack would take them by surprise and catch them in disorder, terrifying them more in the dark. But others were also listening to the conversation, and so Alexander answered that it was disgraceful to steal victory, and that an Alexander must win openly and without trickery. This high-sounding declaration did not look so much like mere vanity, but rather showed how confident he was despite the danger; and it seems to me that he was showing simple common sense. For at night many unexpected events happen both to those who are badly prepared for battle and to those who are fully prepared. These can cause the better side to lose and give victory to the weaker, contrary to the expectation of both sides. Although Alexander often took risks in battle, night action seemed too risky. At the same time if Darius were beaten again he would not have to admit that he was a poor general with weak troops if he had been unexpectedly attacked at night. But if any unforeseen disaster befell the Macedonians the enemy would be in friendly country which they knew well, while they themselves would be unfamiliar with the country and entirely surrounded by enemies. A considerable number of these were the prisoners of war who would attack them, not only after a defeat but even if they did not appear to have won decisively. For these reasons I approve of Alexander's decision, and I equally support his bold intention to act openly.

Darius and his army remained all night drawn up in the formation they had first adopted, because they had no regular camp to protect them, and they were afraid that the enemy would attack them during the night. And this, if anything, weakened the Persians' chances at that time; their long stand under arms and the fear which tends to come before great dangers, and which did not strike them suddenly but was brooded on for a long time, demoralised their spirit.

Arrian now sets out the battle formation of the two armies.

When the armies were close together Darius and his personal squadron, the Persian 'Golden Apple' Company – so called from the golden apples on their spear butts – the Indians, Albanians, immigrant Carians and Mardian archers could be clearly seen, drawn up to face Alexander himself and his royal squadron. Alexander led his men at an angle to the right, and the Persians moved to counter him, far outflanking him with their left wing. The Scythian cavalry, riding parallel to him across the front of the battle lines, had already made contact with the troops placed in front of Alexander's main force, but he still led off towards the right, and was now nearly clear of the ground previously levelled by the Persians. At this Darius was afraid that if the Macedonians reached uneven ground his chariots would be useless to him, and so he ordered the troops who were riding ahead of the left wing to wheel

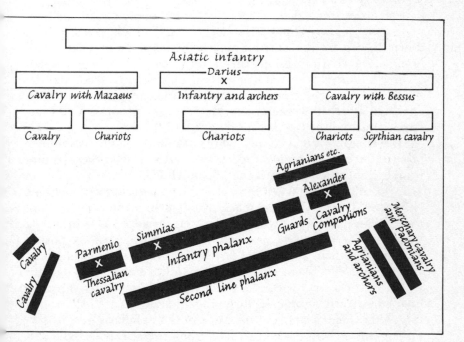

The battle of Gaugamela

39

round the enemy right, led by Alexander, to prevent them extending their line any further. When this happened Alexander ordered his mercenary cavalry, commanded by Menidas, to charge them. The Scythian cavalry and those of the Bactrians who were posted with them made a counter charge, and as they were much superior in numbers they drove Alexander's force back. He then ordered Ariston's squadron, the Paeonians and the mercenaries, to charge the Scythians, and the enemy gave way. However the remaining Bactrians came to grips with the Paeonians and mercenaries, rallied the fugitives on their own side, and brought about a close cavalry action. More men fell on Alexander's side, under pressure from the superior numbers of the enemy, and because the Scythians and their horses had better protective armour. But even so the Macedonians withstood their charges, and falling upon them squadron by squadron broke up their formation.

At this point the enemy launched their scythe-chariots in the direction of Alexander himself in order to disrupt his phalanx. But in this they failed badly; for as soon as they approached, the Agrianians and javelin-throwers commanded by Balacrus, drawn up in front of the Cavalry Companions, met them with volleys of javelins. They also caught hold of the reins, pulled down the drivers, and surrounded the horses and cut them down. Some of the chariots did get through the ranks, but these parted, as they had been told to do, where the chariots attacked, and the result was that the chariots were undamaged and those whom they had attacked were unhurt. However the grooms in Alexander's army and the Royal Guard captured them.

Darius now launched his whole phalanx, while Alexander ordered Aretes to attack the enemy cavalry who were riding round to encircle his right wing. For a while he himself led on his army in column; but when the cavalry who had ridden to help his endangered right wing had to some extent broken up the front of the Persian phalanx, he wheeled towards the gap. Then forming a wedge of the Cavalry Companions and of the phalanx posted there he led them at the double, raising his war-cry, straight at Darius himself. There was a brief hand-to-hand struggle; but when the cavalry with Alexander, and Alexander himself, pressed forward vigorously, thrusting and cutting at the Persians' faces with their spears, and the Macedonian phalanx in close formation and bristling with pikes fell upon them, Darius, who had all along been nervous, saw nothing but danger. He himself was the first to turn and flee. Those Persians who were trying to encircle the Macedonian right were also thrown into a panic when Aretes' men launched a powerful attack.

Here the Persian rout was total and the Macedonians pressed them closely, killing the fugitives. But Simmias' staff and his detachment were unable to join Alexander in the pursuit, and had to halt the phalanx and fight where they were, since the Macedonian left wing was reported to be in difficulty. In fact their line had broken there and some of the Indians and Persian cavalry broke through the gap and pressed on to the Macedonian baggage animals. The struggle at that point was fierce; for the Persians attacked boldly as most of their opponents were unarmed and had never expected anyone to cut through the double phalanx and attack them. The native prisoners of war also joined in the Persian attack on the Macedonians. However the commanders of the troops posted as reserve to the first phalanx, learning what was happening, quickly turned about as they had been ordered and appeared in the rear of the Persians, killing many of them as they crowded round the baggage animals. However some Persians turned and managed to escape.

Meanwhile the Persians on the right wing did not yet know of Darius' flight, and riding round Alexander's left they launched a flank attack on Parmenio's troops. As the Macedonians were at first caught between two fires here, Parmenio sent an urgent message to Alexander that his force was in difficulty and needed help. When Alexander received the message he at once broke off the pursuit, and wheeling round with the Cavalry Companions he led them at the double against the enemy right. First he attacked the enemy cavalry who were already in flight, the Parthyaeans, some of the Indians, and the strongest and best of the Persians. This was the most violent cavalry action of the whole battle. For the Persians who had been drawn up by squadrons now wheeled in column and clashed with Alexander's men head-on. They did not throw javelins nor manoeuvre the horses, as is usual in a cavalry battle, but every man drove against whatever faced him, pressing on as if this were the only hope of safety. They hacked at one another without mercy, no longer fighting for someone else's victory but for their own lives. About sixty of Alexander's Companions fell there, while Hephaestion, Coenus and Menidas were wounded. But Alexander was victorious at that point also. Those of the enemy who broke through Alexander's troops fled at full speed.

Alexander was now on the point of clashing with the right wing of the enemy. But there his Thessalian cavalry had fought brilliantly and were not at all inferior to Alexander in the action. For the enemy right wing was already in flight when Alexander approached. Accordingly he turned away and again began the pursuit of Darius, which he continued as long as daylight lasted. Parmenio's men also pressed on in pursuit of those who had faced them. Alexander crossed the river Lycus and encamped there, to rest his men and horses briefly; but Parmenio captured the enemy camp, baggage animals, elephants and camels.

Alexander rested his cavalry until midnight, and then pressed on rapidly towards Arbela, hoping to capture Darius there with his money and the rest of the royal possessions. On the next day he reached Arbela, having ridden seventy-five miles since the battle. However he did not catch Darius at Arbela, for the king had continued his flight without a rest; but his money and all his possessions were taken, including his chariot, shield and bow for the second time.

About a hundred of Alexander's men had been killed, but over a thousand horses, of which half belonged to the Cavalry Companions, died from wounds and from exhaustion in the pursuit. The Persian dead were reckoned at three hundred thousand, and many more than that were taken prisoner, while the elephants and those chariots which had not been broken up in the battle were also captured. Such was the outcome of this battle, fought in the month of October in the archonship of Aristophanes at Athens [331 B.C.]. Aristander's prophecy had come true, that in the same month in which there was an eclipse of the moon the battle would take place and Alexander would win.

After his victory Alexander's first targets were the great and wealthy cities of the Persian empire. Apart from their treasures their occupation would set the seal on the campaign which had set out to avenge Persia's occupation of Greece, and particularly of Athens, in 480 B.C. At Babylon and Susa Alexander was welcomed by the frightened populations, and in return he behaved properly in every way. In fact he conducted himself as a new king might be expected to do on taking over a throne which had become his. However at Persepolis for some reason the result was different. The city was looted ruthlessly by the soldiers, and the palace was burned by Alexander himself. Arrian reports this as an act of policy, the final symbolic destruction of Persian power. Others less charitably tell of it as the thoughtless result of a drunken orgy.

But occupying cities was not enough; Darius also had to be tracked down. Accordingly the spring of 330 B.C. saw Alexander heading north to Ecbatana and so into Media on his trail. Darius had hoped to raise further forces, but his performance thus far was not likely to attract continued support, and his own companions soon turned against him. To his credit Alexander's treatment of Darius' body and family was entirely appropriate for the ruler of a great empire, and Arrian adds a sympathetic obituary of the king.

At this point Bagistanes, a Babylonian noble from Darius' camp, and Antibelus, one of Mazaeus' sons, came to Alexander. They brought news that Nabarzanes, the commander of the cavalry who had fled with Darius, Bessus, the governor of Bactria, and Barsaentes, the governor of Arachosia and Drangia, had arrested Darius. When he heard this, Alexander pressed on with still greater eagerness, taking with him only the Companions, the scout cavalry, and the toughest and most lightly equipped of his infantry, carefully chosen. He did not even wait for a party with Coenus to return from a foraging expedition. He put Craterus in command of those left behind, with orders to follow, but not by forced marches. His own party had nothing but their weapons and food for two days. After travelling all night and until midday next day he gave his troops a short rest and again pressed on all night. At dawn he reached the camp where Bagistanes had come from. He did not catch the enemy there but learnt the facts about Darius; he had been arrested and was being taken away in a closed waggon, while Bessus had assumed power in his place and had been acknowledged as their leader by the Bactrian cavalry and the other Persians who had fled with Darius, except for Arta-bazus and his sons and the Greek mercenaries. These were loyal to Darius but were unable to prevent what was happening, and so had turned off the main road and were heading for the hills on their own, taking no part in the activities of Bessus and his sup-porters. Those who had arrested Darius intended to hand him over, if they found that Alexander was pursuing them, and so obtain good terms for themselves. But if they heard that Alexan-der had turned back they planned to collect the largest army that they could and combine together to preserve their power. For the time being Bessus was in command, because he was related to Darius and because it was in his province that they had arrested the king.

When Alexander heard this it was clear that he should pursue with all speed. His men and horses were already becoming exhausted by their constant exertion, but even so he led them on, and after a long journey all night, and until midday on the following day, he reached a village where the party with Darius had encamped the day before. When he heard that the Persians had intended to continue their journey during the night he asked the inhabitants if they knew of a shorter route to catch the fugitives. They said they did, but the road was through uninhabited and waterless country. He told them to guide him that way; and realising that his infantry could not keep up with him if he pressed on at speed, he dismounted about five hundred of the cavalry, and choosing the fittest officers of the infantry and other units he ordered them to mount the horses, armed in their usual infantry fashion. He ordered Nicanor, the commander of the Guards, and Attalus, the commander of the Agrianians, to lead the remainder along the route which Bessus' party had taken. They were to travel as lightly equipped as possible, with the rest of the infantry following in their normal formation. He himself set off at dusk and pressed ahead at speed. After covering fifty miles in the night he came upon the Persians at dawn. They were travelling in disorder and unarmed, so that only a few of them turned to resist; the majority fled without coming to grips as soon as they saw Alexander. Those who did turn to fight also fled when a few were killed. Bessus and his supporters still had Darius with them in the waggon, but when Alexander caught up with them Nabarzanes and Barsaentes wounded Darius and abandoned him there, themselves fleeing with six hundred cavalry. Darius died from his wounds a little before Alexander arrived to see him.

Alexander sent Darius' body to Persepolis, with orders for its burial in the royal tombs as the previous kings had been. He appointed Amminaspes, a Parthyaean, as governor of the Parthyaeans and Hyrcanians; he was one of those who, along with Mazaeus, had surrendered Egypt to Alexander. Tlepolemus, the son of Pythophanes, one of the Companions, was appointed along with him to supervise affairs in Parthyaea and Hyrcania.

Such was the death of Darius, in the month of July when Aristophon was archon in Athens [330 B.C.]. In matters of warfare he was the weakest and most incompetent of men, but in other ways he did nothing unreasonable, or at any rate he had no chance to do so, because he happened to come to the throne at the very time when war was declared by the Macedonians and the Greeks. Even if he had wished, it was never possible for him to behave tyrannically towards his subjects, for he was in greater danger than they. In his lifetime he suffered one disaster after another, and he had had no respite from the first moment when he came to power. At once there befell the cavalry defeat of his governors at the Granicus, and straight away Ionia, Aeolia, both Phrygias, Lydia and Caria except for Halicarnassus fell into enemy hands. A little later Halicarnassus was taken too and the whole coast as far as Cilicia. Then followed his own defeat at Issus, where he saw his mother, wife and children taken prisoner. After that Phoenicia and all Egypt was lost; he himself was the first to flee, shamefully, at Gaugamela, and he lost the greatest army of the whole Persian nation. Thereafter he wandered as a fugitive from his own kingdom, and was at last utterly betrayed by his own companions. King and prisoner at the same time he was led off in total dishonour, and at last was killed by a conspiracy of those most closely associated with him. This is what happened to Darius in his lifetime. But when he was dead, he was buried in the royal tomb, and his children received the upbringing and education from Alexander which they would have had if their father had remained king, while Alexander married his daughter. He was about fifty years old when he died.

4   Plots and intrigues at court

Alexander's campaign had now reached a turning point. With Darius dead and the great Persian cities taken, men may have felt that the expédition was over. But Alexander now saw wider visions before him. He would secure his rule permanently, and that required the conquest of the more easterly areas of the empire and the defeat of the remaining Persian governors. At the same time he had to make plans to rule the lands recently conquered. He saw well enough that he could not hold down such an empire by force. He did not have the manpower to control so vast an area. He must rather work with his new subjects, use their nobles, and win their loyalty. From this point strains begin to show in his relationship with his old comrades. If he promoted a native they were jealous, if he showed respect for native traditions they were puzzled and hurt. From now on this problem of governing such different peoples becomes a fundamental part of the story.

Before long the first crisis arose. After operations to the south of the Caspian Sea Alexander pushed on to the fringes of Bactria only to learn of a plot against his life, involving one of the highest officers in his army, Philotas, the commander of the Cavalry Companions. It appears that Philotas had been told of a plot which he did not reveal to Alexander. His informant, finding that the story was not passed on, found other means of getting word to the king. The plotters were liquidated, and Philotas' silence naturally brought him under great suspicion too. He was put on trial and found guilty. But his death could not end the affair. His father, the veteran general Parmenio, was at Ecbatana, with a force nearly as large as Alexander's own. Had he chosen to rebel, as the news of his son's death might have provoked him to do, the situation would have been desperate. Alexander unhesitatingly arranged his death, or more accurately his murder. We can only guess at the tremors which ran through the army. Some late accounts are lurid indeed (the Roman writer Curtius devoted seven chapters to it), but Arrian remains very brief and matter-of-fact.

At Zarangia, Alexander learnt of the plot of Philotas the son of Parmenio. Ptolemaeus and Aristoboulus say that he had previously been told of it in Egypt, but he had thought it impossible, because Philotas was an old friend and because Alexander had given honour to his father, and had shown his personal friendship to him. Ptolemaeus, the son of Lagus, says that Philotas was brought before the Macedonians; Alexander accused him vigorously and Philotas made his defence. Those who had exposed the plot came forward and brought various clear proofs against Philotas and his associates. In particular they showed that Philotas himself admitted knowing of a plot formed against Alexander, but he was proved to have made no mention of it to Alexander, although he visited his tent twice a day. Philotas and the others who were implicated in the plot with him were shot down with javelins by the Macedonians. Alexander sent Polydamas, one of the Companions, to deal with Parmenio, with a letter to Cleander, Sitalces and Menidas, the generals in Media; for they had been appointed to serve with the army which Parmenio commanded. Parmenio was killed by them, because Alexander was convinced that if Philotas were plotting, Parmenio would have had a share in his son's plans. Moreover even if he had not been involved, had he survived Parmenio would have been a threat, since his son had been executed and he himself was a man of high prestige, both with Alexander and with the rest of the army, not only the Macedonians but also the mercenaries. For he had often commanded them, both in the course of duty and on special missions, appointed by Alexander and with Alexander's full approval.

Alexander's target now was Bessus, the usurper of Darius. In the spring of 329 B.C. the army pushed on through Bactria and across the river Oxus. It was not long before Bessus was in Alexander's hands, but even Arrian is roused to criticism by the fate of the prisoner.

After crossing the river Oxus Alexander led his men at full speed to where he had heard that Bessus and his force were. Meanwhile messengers arrived from Spitamenes and Dataphernes to say that if an army, even if it were only a small one, and a responsible officer were sent they would arrest Bessus and hand him over to Alexander; even now they were keeping him under open arrest. When he heard this Alexander rested his army, leading it on more slowly than before; but he sent Ptolemaeus the son of Lagus with three units of the Cavalry Companions, all the mounted javelin-throwers, Philotas' infantry brigade, one regiment of the Guards, all the Agrianians and half the archers. Their orders were to press on with all speed to find Spitamenes and Dataphernes.

Ptolemaeus went as he was ordered, and after covering ten

normal days' journey in four days he reached the camp where the Persians with Spitamenes had been encamped the day before. There he learnt that Spitamenes and Dataphernes were not firm in their decision to give up Bessus. Accordingly, he left the infantry with orders to follow him in proper formation, and himself rode ahead with the cavalry until he came to a village where Bessus and a few soldiers were. Spitamenes and his party had already left the place, as conscience had made them shrink from giving up Bessus. Ptolemaeus posted his cavalry all round the village, for it was a walled settlement with gates, and made an announcement to the inhabitants that they could go away unharmed if they gave up Bessus. Accordingly, they admitted Ptolemaeus and his men into the village, and he arrested Bessus and withdrew. He then sent to Alexander to ask how he should bring Bessus into his presence. Alexander told him to strip him naked, put a wooden collar on him, and stand him on the right of the road where he and the army were going to pass; and this is what Ptolemaeus did.

When Alexander saw Bessus he stopped his chariot and asked him why he had first arrested Darius, his king, relation and benefactor, then led him away in chains, and eventually killed him. Bessus answered that he had not done it on his own initiative alone, but in agreement with Darius' party at that time, to win safety for themselves from Alexander. At that Alexander ordered him to be flogged, and during the flogging a crier was to repeat the same words of reproach which Alexander had used when he was questioning Bessus. After this degrading punishment Bessus was sent to Bactria to be executed. This is Ptolemaeus' account of the treatment of Bessus; but Aristoboulus says that it was the followers of Spitamenes and Dataphernes who brought Bessus to Ptolemaeus and handed him over to Alexander naked and wearing the collar.

> Although this description suggests that Bessus had already been
> sent off for execution this may not have been so. A few chapters later
> another version of his death is recounted, and the manner of it leads
> Arrian to express his doubts about the way Alexander had begun to
> behave.

Alexander then called a conference of those with him and brought Bessus before them. After accusing him of his betrayal of Darius he ordered his nose and the tips of his ears to be cut off. He was then taken to Ecbatana to be executed there before the assembled

Medes and Persians. I personally do not approve of this excessive punishment of Bessus. I regard mutilation of the extremities as a barbaric practice, and I admit that Alexander was led to copy Median and Persian extravagance, and the habit of barbaric kings of treating their subjects as inferior beings. Nor do I at all approve that he, a descendant of Heracles, began to wear Median instead of traditional Macedonian dress. Similarly he felt no shame in assuming the head-dress of the defeated Persians instead of what he, their conqueror, had always worn. I do not approve of any of this, but I count Alexander's great achievements as proof, if anything is, that neither physical strength, nor noble birth, nor success in war even greater than Alexander's, is of any use to make a man happy. If anyone sailed round Libya and Asia, as Alexander planned to do, and conquered them both, if he added Europe to them to give three parts to his empire, he would be no happier, despite these supposedly great achievements, if he did not have control over himself.

. . . .

Nearly two years of dangerous campaigning followed against the tribesmen of Bactria and Sogdiana. The country was difficult, supplies hard to come by, and the enemy not easy to pin down. Guerilla warfare had to be the order of the day. But it was at Samarcand in the autumn of 328 B.C. that there occurred one of the most disgraceful episodes in Alexander's career, his killing of Cleitus, now joint commander of the Cavalry Companions, in a drunken rage. Arrian does his best to find a better side to the story.

It will not be out of place here to tell of the death of Cleitus, the son of Dropides, and how Alexander reacted after it, even if it did happen a little later. The Macedonians used to keep a day holy to Dionysus, and every year on that day Alexander sacrificed to this god. But they say that on this occasion he neglected Dionysus and decided for some reason or other to sacrifice to the Dioscuri. When the drinking had been going on for a long time (for Alexander had also been converted to barbaric excess in his drinking habits) there was some discussion of the Dioscuri, and how their parentage was no longer attributed to Tyndareus but to Zeus. Then, in flattery of Alexander, some of those present, the sort of people who have always harmed the interests of kings, and will never cease harming them, said that they thought there was no comparison between Alexander and his achievements and those of Castor and Pollux. In their drunken state some did not even stop short of criticising Heracles. They said that only envy prevented living people from receiving the honour they deserved from their contemporaries.

Now Cleitus had obviously been upset for a long time by Alexander's change to more barbaric habits and by what his flatterers were saying. He too was under the influence of drink, and he said that he could not let them offend the divine powers nor belittle the deeds of heroes of the past simply to do Alexander a favour which was in fact no favour at all. Nor were Alexander's achievements as great and wonderful as their exaggerated remarks suggested. In fact, he had not achieved them on his own, but for the most part they were the work of the Macedonians.

What he said upset Alexander, and I myself cannot approve of his words. For I think that in a drinking party of this sort a man should simply keep quiet about his own opinion and not join in the same flattery as the others. But when some recalled Philip's achievements and said, again trying to please Alexander, that they were not particularly remarkable – a view which was quite unjust – Cleitus, no longer in control of himself, spoke up on Philip's behalf and belittled Alexander and his achievements. Under the influence of the wine he was full of criticism of Alexander, and added that he himself had saved Alexander during the cavalry battle against the Persians on the river Granicus. Proudly holding up his right hand he said, 'This is the hand that saved you then, Alexander.'

Alexander could no longer bear Cleitus' drunken insults and jumped up in his anger to strike him, but was held back by the others in the party. However Cleitus did not stop abusing him. Alexander shouted out, calling for the Guards; and when no one paid attention he cried that he had come to the same state as Darius, when he was led off by Bessus and his friends, and that he had nothing left of his kingship but the name. His friends were no longer able to hold him, but some say that he leapt up, seized a spear from one of his bodyguard, and with it struck Cleitus dead. Others say that he snatched a pike from one of his bodyguards and used that. Aristoboulus does not record the circumstances of the drinking party, but he puts the blame on Cleitus alone. He says that when Alexander lost his temper and jumped up to kill him, Cleitus was taken out of the door and over the wall and ditch of the citadel where this was happening by Ptolemaeus, son of Lagus, one of the bodyguard. But he could not control himself and went back, and he met Alexander just as he was calling for him. 'Here I am, Alexander. I am Cleitus,' he said, and at once was struck dead with the pike.

I strongly blame Cleitus for his insulting behaviour towards his king, and I sympathise with Alexander for what happened, because he showed that he was subject to two vices, anger and drunkenness. It is of course not right for any self-respecting man to be overcome by either of these. But I admire Alexander for what happened next, for he at once recognised that he had done a terrible thing. Some say that he leaned the pike against the wall and intended to throw himself upon it, because it was not right for a man who had killed his friend through drunkenness to live. But most writers do not give that story; they say that Alexander went and lay weeping on his bed, calling Cleitus' name and the name of Cleitus' sister, Lanice, who had been his own nurse. What a fine return had he repaid her for her nursing when he had grown up. She had seen her sons die fighting for him, and he had killed her brother with his own hand! He repeatedly called himself the murderer of his friends, and for three days went without food and drink, paying no attention at all to his bodily needs.

Some of the priests said that this had happened because Dionysus was angry with Alexander for neglecting his sacrifice. Eventually Alexander was persuaded by his friends, though with difficulty, to take food, and he reluctantly began to pay attention to his bodily needs. Then he made the sacrifice to Dionysus, since he was not sorry to see what had happened blamed on the god rather than his own wickedness. But in all this I admire Alexander very much, because he did not try to justify his crime, nor make it worse by defending and excusing the guilt, but admitted that being an ordinary human being he had done wrong.

Arrian follows this story closely with an account of further disputes over Alexander's increasing tendency to encourage Persian customs, and the story of another plot on his life. This probably occurred a year later, but Arrian treats it out of order because of its similarity of subject. Callisthenes was Alexander's official historian, and a pupil of the great scholar Aristotle, but clearly a tactless and foolish man. He is recorded as having said that but for the history which he would write, Alexander and his work would soon be forgotten. Rather, Callisthenes himself would have been forgotten but for his own stupidity in provoking Alexander. And yet the issue over which they quarrelled, whether or not men should bow down before Alexander, divided the court. To a freedom-loving Greek it was an intolerable sign of oriental despotism, to Alexander's new eastern subjects a man who did not accept it was hardly worth their respect as a king.

The following story is told of how Callisthenes opposed Alexander on the question of bowing down to him. Alexander had agreed with the scholars and the most distinguished of the Persians and Medes at his court that this subject should be mentioned during a drinking party. Anaxarchus began the conversation by saying that it was much more reasonable for them to regard Alexander as a god than Dionysus or Heracles. This was not just because of Alexander's many remarkable achievements, but also because Dionysus was a Theban, who had no connection with the Macedonians, and Heracles was an Argive, equally unconnected with them except by a family link through Alexander; for Alexander was a descendant of Heracles. The Macedonians would be more justified in treating their own king with divine honours. Of course there was no doubt that when he left the world of men, they would honour him as a god. How much more reasonable it was to honour him when he was still alive, rather than when he was dead and would find no benefit in it.

When Anaxarchus had spoken in this way for a while those who were in the know supported him, and in fact were anxious to set the example of bowing down. Most of the Macedonians disagreed and kept quiet, but Callisthenes interrupted and said,

'Anaxarchus, I do not think that Alexander is unfit for any honour that is proper for a man. But we have always distinguished in many ways between honours suitable for men and those suitable for gods. We build temples for gods, set up their statues, set aside sacred ground, offer sacrifices and drink offerings, and we compose hymns to them. For men we write words of praise. But the main distinction is in the custom of bowing down. Men receive a kiss from those who greet them, but a god is set far above us and it is not permitted to touch him, and so he is honoured by our bowing down to him. Similarly, dances are held in honour of the gods and hymns are sung to them. Nor is this surprising, since among the gods themselves different honours are granted, and different ones again for heroes, quite distinct from those for gods. So it is not right to confuse all these, raising men to an excessive level by exaggerated honours, and degrading the gods, in so far as one can, to an improper humiliation, by honouring them in the same way as men. Alexander would not tolerate it if some private citizen were admitted to royal honours by an unlawful election or vote. With much more reason will the gods be angry if men promote themselves to divine honours, or allow themselves to be promoted by others.

'Alexander is, and is known to be, incomparably the bravest of brave men, the most kingly of kings, the most worthy of generals to hold command. You, Anaxarchus, if anyone, should have taken the lead in saying what I am saying and in arguing against the opposite view, for you are in Alexander's company specifically to guide him in wisdom. It was not right for you to start the conversation as you did. You should have remembered that you are not the attendant or adviser of a Cambyses or a Xerxes, but of a son of Philip, a descendant of Heracles and Aeacus, whose ancestors came from Argos to Macedonia and maintained their rule not by force but by law. Not even Heracles himself received divine honours from the Greeks when he was still alive, nor even when he was dead, until the god at Delphi proclaimed that they should honour him as a god.

'On the other hand, if we must think like foreigners because our discussion is taking place in a foreign land, I still think that you should remember Greece, Alexander. For her sake you undertook the whole expedition, to add Asia to Greece. Think of this too; when you go back home will you even force the Greeks, the greatest freedom-lovers of all, to bow down to you? Or will you let the Greeks off but still impose this shame on the Macedonians? Or will you make a general distinction in the matter of honours, so that by Greeks and Macedonians you will be honoured as a man, and only by foreigners in the foreign way? It may be said of Cyrus, the son of Cambyses, that he was the first man to allow others to bow down to him, and that as a result this shameful way of behaving became normal among Persians and Medes. But you must remember that the Scythians, a poor but independent people, humiliated Cyrus. Other Scythians did the same to Darius, the Athenians and Spartans humbled Xerxes, Clearchus and Xenophon with their ten thousand men brought down Artaxerxes, and Alexander, without men bowing down to him, has now humiliated Darius.'

By these and similar remarks Callisthenes upset Alexander a great deal, but what he said pleased the Macedonians. Alexander realised this and told the Macedonians not to think of bowing down to him in future. Silence fell at these words, and then the senior Persians stood up and bowed down in turn before him. Leonnatus, one of the Companions, thought that one of the Persians bowed in an ungainly way and laughed at his undignified attitude. At the time Alexander was angry with him, but they were reconciled later.

Another similar story is recorded as well. Alexander passed round a golden cup, first to those with whom he had made the arrangement to discuss the question of bowing down. The first drank from the cup, rose from his seat, bowed down to Alexander and received a kiss from him. All the others in turn did the same. But when it was Callisthenes' turn to drink he stood up, drank from the cup and went forward, expecting to kiss Alexander without first bowing down. Alexander happened to be talking to Hephaestion at the time and did not notice whether Callisthenes had carried out the act of bowing down. But Demetrius, the son of Pythonax, one of the Companions, commented as Callisthenes came forward to give the kiss that he had not bowed down. At that Alexander did not allow him to kiss him, and Callisthenes remarked, 'Then I shall go away a kiss worse off.'

I cannot approve of these stories at all, as they reflect upon the arrogance of Alexander at that time and the rudeness of Callisthenes. But I maintain that when a man has undertaken to serve a king he should behave in a proper manner, while advancing the king's cause as far as he can. So I do not think that it was unreasonable for Alexander to be angry with Callisthenes for his misplaced outspokenness and his stupid conceit. For the same reason I imagine that people were ready to believe those who accused Callisthenes of being involved in the plot which was made against Alexander by his boy attendants. Some even say that Callisthenes himself put them up to it.

.   .   .   .

The story of the Pages' Plot is an appropriate sequel to this chapter. Again Alexander was lucky to survive, but, despite these plots and the flaws of character which Alexander was beginning to show, he retained the massive loyalty, and indeed devotion, of the army as a whole.

It had been established by Philip that the sons of Macedonian nobles, when they had reached adolescence, should be chosen as personal attendants on the king. Their duties included general care of his person and guarding him when he was asleep. Whenever the king went riding they collected the horses from the grooms, brought them to him and helped him to mount, in Persian fashion, and they joined in with the king in the rivalry of the hunt. Hermolaus, the son of Sopolis, was one of these young men. He had a reputation for an interest in philosophy, and because of this he was an associate of Callisthenes. There is a story about him that in a hunt, when a boar charged Alexander, Hermolaus aimed and hit the boar before Alexander could. The boar fell dead, but Alexander was furious with Hermolaus, because he had himself missed the chance, and in anger he ordered him to be flogged while the other boys watched, and he deprived him of his horse.

Hermolaus, deeply angry at the insult, told Sostratus the son of Amyntas, a close friend of his own age, that life was not worth living if he could not have his revenge on Alexander for this treatment. He easily persuaded Sostratus, because they were very close friends, to help in what he wanted to do. They then persuaded Antipater the son of the former governor of Syria Asclepiodorus, Epimenes the son of Arseus, Anticles the son of Theocritus, and Philotas the son of Carsis the Thracian to join them. They agreed to attack Alexander and kill him in his sleep on the night when Antipater's turn to be on guard came round.

Now it happened that on that night Alexander continued drinking until dawn. Some say that this was pure chance, but Aristoboulus has recorded that a Syrian woman who had the power to foretell the future kept following Alexander. At first Alexander and his friends laughed at her, but when everything that she forecast turned out to be true Alexander no longer ignored her; she was allowed to see the king day and night, and often watched over him when he was asleep. So on this occasion, in the grip of divine inspiration, she met Alexander when he was leaving the drinking party, and begged him to go back and drink all night. Alexander was convinced that this was a message from the gods, and he went back and continued drinking, and so the boys' plot failed.

On the next day Epimenes the son of Arseus, one of those involved in the plot, told Charicles the son of Menander, who was a close friend of his, and Charicles told Eurylochus, Epimenes' brother. Eurylochus then went to Alexander's tent and told the king's bodyguard, Ptolemaeus the son of Lagus, the whole story. He passed it on to Alexander. Alexander ordered all whom Eurylochus had named to be arrested. Under torture they admitted their plot and also named some other conspirators as well. Aristoboulus says they claimed that Callisthenes had urged them to risk the crime, and Ptolemaeus records the same. But most witnesses do not agree with that, and simply say that Alexander readily believed the worst of Callisthenes because he already hated him, and because Hermolaus was closely associated with Callisthenes.

Some writers have also recorded that when Hermolaus was brought before the Macedonians he admitted the plot, for he said it was no longer possible for a free man to tolerate the arrogance of Alexander. He listed all his grievances, the unjust death of Philotas, the still more illegal killing of his father Parmenio and the others who were executed at that time, the drunken murder of Cleitus, his wearing of Persian dress, the intention which he had not yet denied of making people bow down before him, his drinking bouts and consequent need to sleep it off. He declared that he was not prepared to tolerate this and had resolved to free himself and the other Macedonians.

Hermolaus and those arrested with him were stoned to death by the by-standers. Aristoboulus also records that Callisthenes was put in chains and led about with the army like that until he fell ill and died. Ptolemaeus the son of Lagus says that he was tortured and executed by hanging. Thus even quite reliable historians, who were with Alexander at the time, have not given the same account of notorious events which could not have been unknown to them. Also writers have differed in many other points of detail of these events, but what I have written will have to be sufficient. It actually happened a little later, but I have recorded it after the story of Cleitus and Alexander as I thought the subject was connected.

5   The eastern frontier

In the spring of 327 B.C. Alexander was still campaigning in Sogdiana. Here the native strongholds were built on hills, more difficult to assault than the walled cities of Greece and Persia. Yet this
merely gave Alexander another opportunity to show how the army
could be roused to great feats by the inspiration of his leadership.
The capture of the Rock of Sogdiana also brought him a bride, the
daughter of a Bactrian chief.

At the beginning of spring, Alexander advanced towards the
Rock of Sogdiana, where he had been told that many of the
natives had fled. The wife and daughters of Oxyartes the Bactrian
were also said to have taken refuge there, because Oxyartes had
himself revolted against Alexander and had sent them to the
Rock, thinking it could never be captured. It was clear that if the
Rock were taken there would no longer be any place of refuge left
for those of the natives who wished to revolt. When they
approached the Rock Alexander discovered that it was sheer
against attack on every side, and that the natives had stocked up
with provisions for a long siege. A great deal of snow had also
fallen and made the climb more difficult for the Macedonians,
while giving the natives freedom from any anxiety about their
water supply. Even so Alexander decided to attack. For he had
been roused to anger and provoked to prove his worth by an
insulting remark from one of the natives: when he had invited
them to a conference, and had offered them the chance to withdraw safely to their homes, on condition that they hand over the
position, they had let out a shout of barbaric laughter and told
him to look for soldiers who could fly to capture the hill for him;
they had no worry about anyone else. As a result Alexander
announced that he would give a reward of twelve talents to the
first of his men to reach the top, eleven to the second, ten to the
third, and so on down to one talent for the twelfth. The men were
already eager, and this proclamation excited them even more.

About three hundred men were assembled, who had had practice in rock-climbing during earlier sieges. They had prepared
small iron pegs, with which the tents were normally pegged

down, intending to drive them into the snow where it was frozen, and also into the ground bare of snow. They secured these to strong linen ropes and set off at night up the most sheer and so least guarded part of the cliff. By fixing these pegs into the ground where it was visible, or into those patches of snow which were least likely to give way, they hauled themselves by various routes up the cliff face. About thirty of them were killed in the ascent, and their bodies could not even be found and buried as they had fallen into the snow in different places. But the rest reached the top by dawn, occupied the summit of the mountain, and signalled to the Macedonian camp with linen flags, as Alexander had ordered. He then sent a herald and told him to shout to the native guards not to waste any more time, but to surrender; for the flying soldiers had been found and the summit of the mountain was in his hands. At the same time he pointed to the soldiers at the top.

The natives were amazed at the unexpected sight. Assuming that the men occupying the summit were more numerous than they really were, and properly armed as well, they surrendered; for they were so frightened by the sight of those few Macedonians. Many of their wives and children were also captured, notably the wife and daughters of Oxyartes. Now one of Oxyartes' daughters was a girl of marriageable age called Roxane. Those who served with Alexander say that she was the most beautiful of the Asian women they saw, except for Darius' wife. As soon as he saw her, Alexander fell in love with her, but great as his passion was he was unwilling to treat her with force while she was only a prisoner; but he did not think it out of place to marry her. For this act of Alexander's, I have more praise than blame.

. . . .

From Sogdiana Alexander fought his way across the Hindu Kush and through the Kabul Valley towards India. To the north-east of the Khyber Pass, in a bend of the Indus River, rises the Rock of Aornos. At first reading Arrian's account of its capture seems impossible. No man and no army could achieve such things. But archaeology has proved it. The site is as Arrian describes, and Alexander virtually redesigned the landscape in order to make the hill accessible. We can only marvel at the determination of the soldiers, and their sheer toughness in achieving such an amazing feat, not at leisure, not in cold blood, but in the teeth of the enemy, and with only such resources as they could assemble on the spot.

When the people of Bazira heard what Alexander was doing they lost all hope, and at midnight they abandoned the town. The other natives did the same, and leaving their cities they all took refuge on a cliff in the area, called Aornos. This is a very remarkable rock, and the story goes that it could not even be captured by Heracles the son of Zeus. I cannot state firmly whether the Theban Heracles, or the Tyrian or the Egyptian actually came to India. I am inclined to think that he did not, but that whenever things are difficult men exaggerate their difficulty by spreading the story that even Heracles could not do them. So my opinion about this rock is that Heracles was brought into the story to make it more impressive. They say that the circumference of the rock is twenty-five miles, that its height excluding the peak is nearly seven thousand feet, and that there is only one way up, a difficult track cut from the rock. There is a good supply of pure water on the top, a spring streaming down, and wood and good land for cultivation sufficient for a thousand men to work on. When Alexander heard this he was very anxious to capture the mountain, especially because of the story about Heracles.

> Alexander established control of the neighbouring country and marched towards the mountain.

When Alexander came to Embolima, a city near the Rock of Aornos, he left Craterus there with part of the army, with orders to collect as many provisions as he could, and anything else needed for a long stay. The Macedonians would use that camp as a base to wear down the occupants of the rock by a long siege, if they could not capture it by direct attack. He himself took the archers, the Agrianians, Coenus' brigade, and the lightest yet best armed of the rest of the phalanx. He added to these two hundred of the Cavalry Companions and one hundred mounted archers, and so approached the rock. On the first day he encamped in what seemed a convenient spot, and on the next day he went a little closer to the rock and encamped again.

Some of the neighbouring tribesmen now came to see him. They put themselves in his hands, and said that they would lead him to the most vulnerable part of the rock, which he could use as the starting point to capture it easily. Alexander sent Ptolemaeus the son of Lagus, his bodyguard, with them, in command of the Agrianians and the other light infantry and picked men from the Guards. His orders were to seize the position, hold it with a strong garrison, and signal that it was in his hands. Ptolemaeus went by a rough and difficult track and occupied the position unseen by

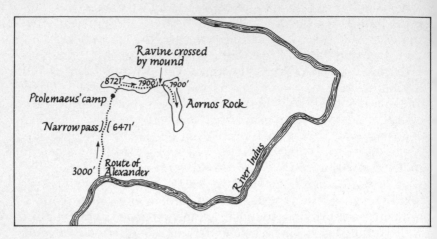

Alexander's approach to Aornos

the natives. He secured it with a stockade and ditch all round, and raised a fire signal from a high spot where Alexander was sure to see it. The signal was seen immediately, and on the next day Alexander led the army forward, but as the natives resisted he made no progress because of the difficult ground. When the natives saw that Alexander could not advance they turned back and attacked the party with Ptolemaeus. A fierce battle took place between them, as the Indians strove to tear down the stockade and Ptolemaeus made every effort to hold the position. The natives had the worst of it in the exchange of missile fire and withdrew when night fell.

Alexander then chose an Indian deserter whom he could trust and who knew the area, and sent him to Ptolemaeus in the night taking a letter. He had written that as soon as he himself attacked the rock, Ptolemaeus was to charge down on the natives from his higher position, and not merely to be satisfied with holding it, so that the Indians would be under fire from both sides. At dawn he broke camp and led the army up the ascent which Ptolemaeus had originally climbed unnoticed. He felt that if he could force his way up there and join Ptolemaeus' party the action would become simple. So it turned out. There was a fierce battle between the Macedonians and the Indians, as the one party tried to force the ascent and the others bombarded them as they climbed. But as the Macedonians did not waver, coming up group after group while those in front rested as support joined them, at dusk they gained control of the way, though with difficulty, and joined Ptolemaeus' group. From there the united army again assaulted the rock itself, but the attempt was still unsuccessful. That was the end of their efforts on that day.

At dawn Alexander ordered each soldier to cut a hundred stakes. When these were cut he ordered them to build a huge mound, starting from the crest of the hill where they had camped, up to the rock. From there he thought that arrows and missiles fired from the siege engines could reach the defenders. They all tackled the work of building the mound with a will, while Alexander himself stood by to supervise and to praise any who worked with extra enthusiasm, or to punish any who were negligent.

On the first day the army built a mound over six hundred feet long. On the next, the slingers used their slings against the Indians from the part already built, while the missiles fired from the siege engines checked Indian attacks on those working on the mound. In three days the mound was completely finished. On the fourth a few of the Macedonians forced their way forward and occupied a small hill on a level with the rock itself. Alexander did not hesitate, but began to extend the mound, wanting to link it to the hill which that party was now holding.

The Indians were appalled at this unimaginable act of daring by the Macedonians who had forced their way onto the hill. When they saw the mound complete they gave up any attempt at defence, but sent a messenger to Alexander to say that they were willing to give up the rock if he would negotiate terms. They had made a plan to spin out the discussion of the terms all day and to scatter to their separate tribes in the night. Alexander discovered this, and so gave them time to withdraw and to remove their complete circle of sentries. He waited until they had begun to retreat, and then taking seven hundred of his bodyguard and of the Guards he climbed up to the part of the rock which they had abandoned, and was himself the first to reach it. The other Macedonians followed, hauling each other up. Then at a given signal they turned upon the retreating natives and killed many of them as they fled. Some, in the terror of their retreat, threw themselves over the cliffs and so died.

Thus the rock which Heracles had found impossible fell to Alexander. He held a sacrifice upon it and posted a garrison, putting in command Sisicottus, an Indian who had once come to Bactria and deserted to Bessus; but when Alexander took Bactria

61

Sisicottus joined him and proved himself absolutely reliable.

.   .   .   .

Alexander was now approaching India and perhaps the greatest of
his battles. King Porus was no weak ruler like Darius, nor was the
Hydaspes – the modern river Jhelum – a comparatively modest
stream such as the Granicus or Pinarus. Moreover Indian war elephants, although met in small numbers in the last few months, were
a new threat as a massed force in a set battle. But Alexander liked
nothing better than a challenge, and the story is yet another tribute
to his determined leadership and the loyalty and toughness of his
men.

Alexander had been told that Porus was on the far bank of the
Hydaspes with his whole army, determined to prevent his crossing or to attack him if he tried. When he heard this, Alexander
sent Coenus, the son of Ptolemocrates, back to the Indus with
orders to take to pieces the boats which he had used to cross that
river, and to bring them to the Hydaspes. The boats were dismantled and brought, the shorter ones split into two, the thirty-
oared ones into three, and so the sections were transported on
carts to the bank of the Hydaspes. There the ships were re-
assembled and were now to be seen all together on the river. Alexander himself took the forces with which he had come to Taxila,
plus five thousand Indians under the command of Taxiles and the
local chiefs, and advanced to the Hydaspes.

Alexander encamped on the river bank, and Porus could be
seen opposite him with his whole army and his force of elephants.
Porus stayed and personally kept guard on the ford where he saw
that Alexander had camped, while he sent guards to other parts of
the river which were suitable for a crossing, with officers in charge
of these parties. He was quite determined to prevent the Macedonians from crossing. But when Alexander saw his preparations
he decided to keep his army constantly on the move, to keep Porus
in doubt. So he split the army into several divisions and himself
led some to various parts of the countryside, partly to destroy
enemy property, partly to look for any place where the river
seemed easy to cross. Other groups were put under various officers whom he similarly sent off in different directions.

Supplies were brought to his camp from all over the countryside on his side of the Hydaspes, so that it was clear to Porus that
Alexander was determined to stay by the river until the water
level dropped in the winter and made it possible for him to cross

in various places. His boats also sailed here and there, skins were filled with chaff to form rafts, and the whole bank was crowded with cavalry and infantry. It was impossible for Porus to rest or to choose one particular spot to guard and concentrate upon that. At that time in particular all Indian rivers were full and turbulent with swift currents. For it was the time of the summer solstice, when heavy rains fall in India, and the snow from the Caucasus, the source of many rivers, melts and raises their level substantially. But in winter they subside and become quite small, clear in appearance, and most rivers, except the Indus, the Ganges, and perhaps one other, are fordable in some places. However the Hydaspes certainly becomes fordable.

Alexander openly said that he would wait for that season of the year if he were prevented from crossing at once. Nevertheless he remained on the alert in the hope that he could seize a chance for a sudden crossing unobserved. However he realised that he could not cross to the part of the river bank where Porus himself was, because of the number of the elephants, and because a large and well-disciplined army, fully equipped, would fall upon his men as they came ashore. The horses also seemed unlikely even to be willing to set foot on the far bank if the elephants attacked them at once, terrifying them by the sight and by the noise they made. In fact the horses probably would not even remain on the rafts during the crossing, but would leap off into the water when they saw the elephants in the distance, and there would be complete panic. So he decided to cross secretly in the following way. Every night he led large parties of cavalry to various points on the bank, made a lot of noise, raised the war-cry, and made every sort of din typical of men preparing to cross. Porus took the elephants and marched along the opposite bank in the direction of the noise, and Alexander got him into the habit of doing this. But when it had been happening for a long time, and nothing but shouting and war-cries came of it, Porus no longer moved his men to match Alexander's cavalry manoeuvres, but thinking that it was a false alarm he stayed in camp where he was.

When Alexander had convinced Porus that there was no cause for alarm about these nightly attempts he contrived the following plan. There was a headland jutting out from the bank at a point where the river bent sharply. This was thickly covered with all sorts of trees, and opposite it was an island in the river, wooded and uninhabited. When Alexander discovered this island opposite the headland, and saw that the wooded nature of the place made it ideal to conceal an attempted crossing, he resolved to take his army over at that point. The headland and the island were about eighteen miles from his main camp. Guards had been posted along the whole bank, close enough together to see each other and to hear easily any order, from wherever it came. During the night, for many nights, shouts were raised in various places and fires were lit. When Alexander had decided to attempt the crossing he made his preparations quite openly in the camp.

Craterus was left in the camp with his own cavalry regiment, the cavalry of the Arachotians and Parapamisadae, the companies of Alcetas and Polysperchon from the Macedonian phalanx, and the chiefs of the Indians in that area with their five thousand men. Craterus was told not to make the crossing until Porus had gone with his army to attack Alexander, or until he knew that Porus was in flight and the Greeks were winning. If Porus took a part of his army to face Alexander, and left a part including elephants in the camp, Craterus was to stay where he was. But if he took all the elephants to oppose Alexander and left some other part of the army in the camp, Craterus was to cross at full speed. For only elephants, Alexander claimed, were a danger to horses as they landed, while the rest of the army would be easy to deal with.

These were Craterus' orders. But between the island and the main camp, where Craterus had been left, Meleager, Attalus and Gorgias had been posted with the mercenary cavalry and infantry. These also had been ordered to cross, dividing their force section by section, when they saw the Indians involved in the battle. Alexander himself chose the crack squadron of the Companions, the cavalry regiments of Hephaestion, Perdiccas and Demetrius, the contingents from Bactria and Sogdiana, the Scythian cavalry, the mounted archers of the Dahae, and, from the phalanx the Guards, the companies of Cleitus and Coenus, the archers and the Agrianians. He led this force unobserved, keeping some distance from the river bank, so as not to be visible while advancing towards the headland and the island where he had decided to cross. There the hide rafts, which had been brought up well in advance, were stuffed with chaff during the night and were carefully sewn up. During that night also there was a violent rainstorm, and because of it Alexander's preparations to attempt the crossing were all the more concealed. The thunder claps and the rain drowned the clatter of weapons and the shouting of orders. Most of the boats which had been dismantled, including the thirty-oared ones, had been brought to that spot, secretly put together again, and hidden in the wood.

Towards dawn the wind dropped and the rain eased. The cavalry force embarked on the rafts while the boats took all the infantry they could, and they crossed to the island, so as not to be seen by the scouts Porus had posted until they had passed the island and were close to the bank. Alexander himself embarked on a thirty-oared boat, with Ptolemaeus, Perdiccas and Lysimachus, members of his bodyguard, and Seleucus, one of the Companions, who later became king, and with half of the Guards. Other thirty-oared boats took the rest of the Guards.

Once the army passed the island they became visible approaching the bank. The scouts saw them coming and galloped to Porus with all the speed their horses could manage. Meanwhile Alexander himself was the first to land. He assembled the men from the thirty-oared boats and drew up the cavalry as they came ashore, for they had been ordered to land first. With them he advanced in battle formation. But because he did not know the country he had landed, without realising it, on another island and not on the mainland. It was a large one, which was why he had not known that it was an island, and was cut off from the mainland only by a small branch of the river. But the violent rain, lasting for much of the night, had raised the water level so that the cavalry could not find the ford, and Alexander was afraid that he would have to face as much trouble as on the first stage of the crossing. When he found a ford he led his men on, difficult though it was; for at its deepest point the water rose over the chests of the infantry, and only the heads of the horses were clear of the water.

When this stream was also crossed Alexander moved the crack cavalry squadron and the best men picked from the other cavalry units onto his right wing. He put the mounted archers in front of the whole cavalry line. Behind the cavalry he placed first the Royal Guards, led by Seleucus, then the Royal Regiment, and close to these the other Guards units in their order of precedence for that day. On both flanks of the phalanx were posted the archers, Agrianians and javelin throwers. With the army in this formation he ordered the infantry, nearly six thousand strong, to follow the cavalry in good order at marching pace. He himself took only the cavalry, numbering about five thousand, and advanced at speed. But he also ordered Tauron, the commander of the archers, to keep pace with the cavalry. His plan was that if Porus' army met him in full force he would either have an easy victory with his cavalry, or he would hold the position until the infantry joined him. But if the Indians were dismayed by the remarkable daring of his crossing and took to flight, he would keep hard on their heels, and the more he could kill in the retreat the less trouble would be left for him.

Aristoboulus records that Porus' son actually arrived with sixty chariots before Alexander made his second crossing from the island. He could have prevented Alexander's crossing, since even unopposed it was difficult, if the Indians had dismounted from their chariots and attacked the first parties to land. But they simply drove past in their chariots and left the crossing unchallenged. Alexander sent his mounted archers to deal with them and easily drove them off, inflicting many wounds. But some writers say that a battle took place at the crossing between the Indians under Porus' son and Alexander leading his cavalry. Porus' son had come with a larger force, and he personally wounded Alexander and inflicted the wound on his beloved horse Bucephalas, from which it died.

Ptolemaeus the son of Lagus, with whom I agree, gives a different version. He also says that Porus sent his son, but not with only sixty chariots. For it was not likely that Porus would have sent his son with a mere sixty chariots if he had heard from his scouts that Alexander himself or part of his army had crossed the Hydaspes. This would have been too large a force for reconnaissance and too inconvenient a size for a quick get-away, but by no means sufficient to prevent an enemy force if it had not yet crossed, or to attack it if it had. Ptolemaeus states that Porus' son arrived with two thousand cavalry and a hundred and twenty chariots, but that Alexander had completed the crossing from the island before he arrived.

Ptolemaeus also says that Alexander first sent his mounted archers against this force, but himself led on the cavalry, supposing that Porus was coming with his whole army and that this cavalry force was his advance party formed up in front of the rest of his army. But when he learned the number of the Indians accurately he attacked them vigorously with his own cavalry. They gave ground when they saw Alexander himself and his massed force of cavalry attacking not on one front but squadron by squadron. About four hundred of the Indian cavalry were killed, including Porus' son, and their chariots and horses were captured in the retreat as they became heavy and useless for action because of the mud.

As soon as the cavalry which had escaped in flight told Porus that Alexander had crossed with his army in full force, and that his son had been killed in the battle, he found himself in two minds. For the force left behind under Craterus, facing him in the main camp, could now be seen attempting to cross. But Porus chose to go against Alexander himself with his full force and to fight it out against the strongest part of the Macedonian army and against their king. Even so he left a few of the elephants and a small part of his army there in the camp, to frighten the cavalry under Craterus, and deter them from approaching the bank. He himself took all his cavalry, about four thousand strong, all his three hundred chariots, two hundred elephants, and the cream of his infantry, numbering thirty thousand men. With this force he advanced against Alexander.

When he came to a spot which did not seem too muddy, but was composed of firm and level sand suitable for the charges and manoeuvres of cavalry he drew up his army. In front were the elephants, about a hundred feet apart, so that their line extended in front of the whole infantry phalanx and would strike fear into Alexander's cavalry at all points. He certainly did not expect that any of the enemy would dare to force their way into the gaps between the elephants. Obviously the cavalry would not do this because the horses would be too frightened, and the infantry were even less likely to attempt it, for they would be checked by the heavy infantry attacking them head on and trampled by the elephants wheeling round upon them. Behind the elephants Porus' infantry were drawn up, not on an equal front with the elephants but in a second line, so that the companies were fitted into the gaps which the elephants left. Porus also had infantry stationed on the flanks extending beyond the elephants. On each flank of these infantry units were cavalry and chariots in front of them.

Such was Porus' formation. But when Alexander saw the Indians forming up he halted his cavalry advance to wait for the infantry units as they continued to arrive. But since his phalanx had come at the double he did not immediately form them up and put tired and breathless troops at the mercy of a fresh enemy by leading them forward as soon as they were all together. Moving his cavalry round the line, he gave the infantry a rest until their spirits were revived. But when he saw how the Indian line was formed he decided not to advance against its centre, where the elephants were posted in the front and the close packed phalanx had filled the gaps between them. He was afraid of exactly what Porus

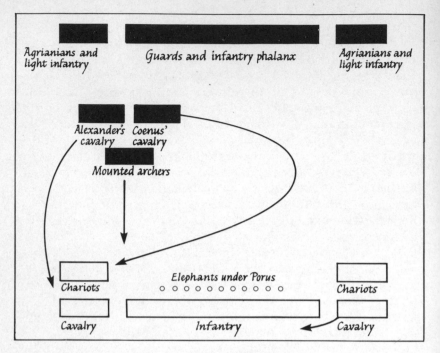

Agrianians and light infantry

Guards and infantry phalanx

Agrianians and light infantry

Alexander's cavalry

Coenus' cavalry

Mounted archers

Chariots

Elephants under Porus
o o o o o o o o o o

Chariots

Cavalry

Infantry

Cavalry

The battle of the Hydaspes

had relied upon when he chose that formation. But because he was superior in cavalry he took the majority of it and rode against the enemy left wing, to launch his attack there. He sent Coenus to the left, with his own and Demetrius' cavalry regiments, with orders to press upon the enemy from the rear once they had been diverted to ride against his own massed cavalry attack. He put Seleucus, Antigenes and Tauron in charge of the infantry phalanx. But they were not to join battle until they saw both the enemy infantry phalanx and cavalry thrown into confusion by his cavalry charge.

Alexander was now in missile range, and he launched his thousand mounted archers at the Indian left, to throw the enemy posted there into confusion by the hail of arrows and the force of the charge. Then he himself with the Cavalry Companions galloped against the enemy left, eager to attack them while they were still in confusion and formed in line, and before they could re-form into mass formation. At the same time the Indians concentrated all their cavalry and rode parallel to Alexander ready to meet his charge. But the force under Coenus could also be seen on their heels as they had been ordered. When the Indians realised this they were forced to divide their cavalry, sending the largest and best group against Alexander while the others wheeled to face Coenus and his force. This at once upset the ranks and plans of the Indians. Alexander saw his chance at the very moment when some of the cavalry were wheeling away, and he attacked the troops opposite him. The Indians did not stand up to Alexander's cavalry charge, but fell back upon the elephants as if to a friendly wall.

At that moment the elephant drivers turned their animals against Alexander's cavalry, while the Macedonian phalanx advanced against the elephants, throwing spears at the drivers, and surrounding and shooting at the animals from all sides. The action was not like any former battle; for the elephants charged into the ranks of infantry, causing destruction wherever they turned among the close formation of the Macedonians. Meanwhile the Indian cavalry, seeing the infantry locked together, wheeled round again and charged the Macedonian cavalry. But when Alexander's men once more got the upper hand, with their great superiority in strength and experience, the Indians again withdrew to the protection of the elephants.

By now all Alexander's cavalry had become concentrated into one body, not from any command but because it had so happened in the course of the fighting. Thus wherever they attacked the Indian ranks they cut them down with great slaughter. The elephants also had become hemmed into a confined space and were doing as much harm to their own side as to the enemy, who were trampled down as the creatures wheeled and charged. In fact it was the Indian cavalry, packed together near the elephants, who suffered the heaviest losses. Many of the elephant drivers had been shot down, some of the elephants had been wounded, and others were out of control because of what was happening to them and for lack of riders. Maddened by pain they charged in every direction, at friend and enemy alike, pushing, trampling and killing. But the Macedonians had plenty of space and could attack the animals when they wanted to, so they fell back when the elephants charged, but closed in and threw their spears when they turned away. The Indians on the other hand were retreating among the elephants, and so were suffering most of their losses from them.

When the animals were tired and their charges were no longer effective, and instead they were merely trumpeting and backing away like ships going astern, Alexander moved his cavalry in a circle round their whole force. He also ordered his infantry to lock their shields into as solid a line as they could, and the whole phalanx was to move forward. So the Indian cavalry were cut down with few survivors. The infantry also were being cut down from all sides as the Macedonians drove home their attack. But as soon as a gap appeared in Alexander's cavalry they all turned and fled through it. At the same time Craterus and the other officers who had been left behind in command of the army on the bank of the Hydaspes saw Alexander winning a decisive victory and themselves began to cross the river. They inflicted just as much slaughter on the retreating Indians, for they joined the pursuit fresh, to replace Alexander's weary troops.

Nearly twenty thousand Indian infantry were killed, as well as three thousand cavalry, and all their chariots were destroyed. Two sons of Porus died, as did Spitaces the local Indian governor, the officers in command of the elephant and chariot forces, and all the cavalry commanders and senior officers. The elephants which had not been killed were captured. Of Alexander's original attacking force of six thousand infantry about eighty died. Ten of the mounted archers who had engaged the enemy first fell, about twenty of the Cavalry Companions, and two hundred of the other cavalry.

Porus had indeed fought manfully in the battle, fulfilling not only the duties of a general but also of an outstanding soldier. When he saw the slaughter of his cavalry, and that some of the elephants had fallen, while others were roaming confused and riderless, and although most of his infantry had been killed, he did not behave as the great king Darius had done. He did not lead the flight of his men, but while any Indians continued fighting he also fought on. But at last he was wounded in the right shoulder, which was the only part of his body which he exposed as he moved about in the battle. For the rest of his body was protected from missiles by his corselet, which was remarkably strong and well-fitting, as those who saw it later could tell. Then he wheeled his elephant and began to retreat.

Alexander had seen what a great and gallant soldier he had shown himself in the battle and was eager to save him. First he sent after him an Indian, Taxiles, who rode as close to Porus' elephant as he thought safe and told him to halt the animal, since it was impossible for him to get away, and to listen to Alexander's message. But when Porus saw Taxiles, who had long been his enemy, he wheeled the elephant and rode at him to attack him with his javelin. In fact he would perhaps have killed him if Taxiles had not anticipated the danger and galloped away. But Alexander was not angry with Porus for this, and sent other messengers in turn, and at last sent an Indian called Meroes, because he knew that he had long been a friend of Porus. When Porus heard Meroes' message, and since he was now also overcome by thirst, he halted the elephant and dismounted. When he had had a drink and felt refreshed he told Meroes to take him quickly to Alexander.

When Alexander heard of his approach he rode out in front of the ranks with a few of the Companions to meet him. As he halted his horse he looked in amazement at Porus' height, over seven feet tall, and at his good looks. Porus did not seem broken in spirit, but like one brave man meeting another, like a king who had fought honourably against another king for his throne. Alexander spoke first and told Porus to say what he wanted to be done with him. The story goes that Porus replied, 'Treat me as a king should, Alexander.' Alexander was delighted by his answer and said, 'It shall be so for my part, Porus. But it is for you to ask what you want.' Porus replied, 'Everything is contained in this one request.' Alexander was even more pleased by this answer and gave back to Porus his rule over the Indians in that area, and added to his former territory an area still greater than he had ruled before. Thus he treated a brave man as a king should, and from that time found him loyal in every way. This was the result of the battle fought against Porus and the Indians on the far side of the Hydaspes in the month of May, during the archonship of Hegemon at Athens [326 B.C.].

It was here that Alexander lost his faithful horse Bucephalas. It would be a pity to omit Arrian's obituary of the horse which rounds off well the story of this great battle. Arrian here contradicts his earlier statement about the wounding of the horse, page 66.

At the place where the battle was fought and the place from which he set off to cross the Hydaspes Alexander founded two cities. He called one Victoria, to commemorate his defeat of the Indians, the other Bucephala in memory of his horse Bucephalas, which died there. It had not suffered any wound but died of exhaustion and age; for it was about thirty years old and worn out. It had shared many toils and dangers with Alexander in earlier days, and was ridden by no one but Alexander, for it would not tolerate

71

any other rider. It was a large horse and noble spirited, branded with the mark of an ox-head from which they say it took its name. But some say that it had a white mark on its head, shaped like the head of an ox, while otherwise it was jet black. This horse had once been lost in Uxia, and Alexander had made an announcement that he would kill every Uxian in the country, if they did not bring back his horse. On the announcement it was at once returned. Such was Alexander's concern for the horse, and such was the fear that he could inspire in the natives. I am glad to record such praise of Bucephalas for Alexander's sake.

> Alexander no longer had any thought of turning back. From the Hydaspes he advanced across two more great rivers, but when he came to a third even his soldiers had had enough. They had been away from home for eight years, they had travelled over eleven thousand miles, and we have only to look at a map to see the sort of country they had crossed, and to read the story to see what acts of courage and feats of sheer hard labour had been involved. Fighting had been almost unbroken and things seemed to be getting harder. Each siege was of a mightier obstacle than the last, each battle against a more powerful and desperate enemy. In the summer of 326 B.C., on the banks of the river Hyphasis, Alexander suffered his only defeat – at the hands of his own men. Nothing he could say or do would persuade them to cross.

Reports stated that the country beyond the river Hyphasis was fertile, while the people were good farmers, brave in war, and had a well-ordered political system. For the most part they were ruled by the upper classes, who did not govern unreasonably. The people in that area had more elephants than the other Indian tribes, which were also particularly large and brave. This news filled Alexander with great enthusiasm to press on. But the Macedonians were now tired of it, as they saw the king moving from one task to another and from one risk to another. Meetings were held in the camp. Even the best men grumbled at their present situation, while others declared that they would not follow even if Alexander led the way. When Alexander heard of this he called together the senior officers, before the confused and despairing mood of the soldiers could get worse, and addressed them:

'Gentlemen of Macedonia and the allies, I can see that you are not following me into danger with your usual spirit, and so I have brought you together to persuade you, and so to lead you on, or to be persuaded by you, and so to turn back. If what we have achieved up to now, and I who have led you, can be criticised, there is no point in my saying anything more. But it is because of these efforts on your part that Ionia is ours; so are the Hellespont and both Phrygias, Cappadocia, Paphlagonia, Lydia, Caria, Lycia, Pamphylia, Phoenicia, Egypt, the Greek part of Libya, parts of Arabia, lowland Syria and Mesopotamia. The people of Susia, the Persians and Medes and the areas which they ruled, not to mention some which they did not, are in our hands. The lands beyond the Caspian Gates, beyond the Caucasus, all that lies across the Tanais, Bactria, Hyrcania and the Caspian Sea have fallen to us. We have driven the Scythians into the desert, the Indus flows through territory which is ours; so do the Hydaspes, the Acesines and the Hydraortes. Why then do you hesitate to add the Hyphasis and the tribes beyond it to your Macedonian empire? Are you afraid that there are other natives who may face up to you when you approach? No; some of them surrender voluntarily, others are caught as they run away, others make their escape and leave their country deserted for you to take, and we give it to our allies and those who have been willing to join us.

'I do not think that a man worth the name looks for any end to tasks that lead to glorious achievement. But if anyone wants to know what the end of this war will be, he can be sure that there is not much land left for us up to the river Ganges and the eastern sea. And I assure you that this sea will be found to join up with the Caspian Sea. For the great sea encircles the whole earth. I will prove to the Macedonians and their allies that the Indian Ocean, the Persian Gulf and the Hyrcanian Sea flow into one another. Our fleet will sail from the Persian Gulf to Libya, right to the Pillars of Heracles. The whole of Libya east of the Pillars is becoming ours, as is the whole of Asia, and the boundaries of our empire are those which god set as the boundaries of the whole world. But if you turn back now many warlike tribes are left between the Hyphasis and the eastern sea, and many more northwards towards the Caspian Sea, while the Scythians are not far away. Thus there is a danger that if we withdraw the areas which are not yet under firm control may rise up, stirred to revolt by those who have not yet been defeated. Then all our labours will have been wasted, or we shall have to tackle all these toils and dangers again from the beginning.

'Stand fast, Macedonians and allies. Glorious achievements come to those who strive and take risks. To live bravely and to leave an everlasting reputation when one dies is true happiness.

Or do you not realise that my ancestor Heracles would not have achieved such glory as to become a god, or to be accepted as one, if he had stayed in Tiryns or Argos and lingered in the Peloponnese or Thebes? Even Dionysus, more fully a god than Heracles was, faced many labours. But we have travelled beyond Nysa, and the Rock of Aornos, which Heracles could not take, is in our hands. Add what still remains of Asia to what you already hold; add that small area to your great conquests! What great and glorious achievements would we have accomplished if we had sat in Macedonia and thought it sufficient to guard our homeland with little effort? What would we have done if we had merely been content to deal with the Thracians on our borders, or the Illyrians and Triballians, or those Greeks who were ill-disposed towards us?

'If while you were suffering and taking risks I myself, your commander, had led you without sharing the same sufferings and risks, you would reasonably have grown tired of it. You would have been undertaking the hard work alone, but gaining the rewards for others. But as it is our hardships are shared, we face the dangers equally, the rewards are open to all. The conquered country is yours; you are its governors. The greatest share of the money comes to you, and when we have overrun Asia then, by Heaven, I will not merely satisfy you; I will go beyond the good things which each of you hopes to gain, and I will either send or personally lead home all who want to go. As for those who stay here, I will make them the envy of those who return home.'

That and more like it was what Alexander said, but a long silence followed. No one dared to argue with him without careful thought, and yet they did not want to accept what he said. Meanwhile Alexander kept telling anyone who wanted to speak to do so, if he really held an opposite view to his own; but the silence lasted for a long time. At last Coenus the son of Polemocrates ventured to make the following reply:

'Your majesty, since you yourself state that you do not want to lead the Macedonians simply by orders, but by convincing them, and you say that failing that you will not compel them, I will make an answer. It is not on behalf of those of us who are here, for we are honoured above the others, and most of us have already received the rewards of our labours and are eager to support you in every way because of our senior authority. No, I will speak on behalf of the majority of the army. Nor will I merely say what pleases them, but what I sincerely think is best for you now and safest for the future. I am entitled to give my opinion openly, both because of my age and because of the reputation which I have among the others, thanks to you, and because of my undeniable courage in our labours and dangers up to now.

'Under your leadership, supported by those who set out with you from home, we have achieved very many great successes. But all the more because of that, I think it is right to set a limit to the tasks we undertake and the risks we run. You yourself see how many Macedonians and Greeks set out with you, and how few of us are left. You sent the Thessalians straight home from Bactria, for you could see that they were no longer enthusiastic to face such labours, and you were right. Some of the other Greeks have been settled in the cities which you have founded, and they are not all staying there willingly. Others, including the Macedonian army, are still facing the work and the dangers with you, but they have lost some of their numbers in battle, while others have been disabled by wounds and left behind in various parts of Asia. More have died of disease, and only a few survive of that first great army, but they are not as vigorous as they were, and they are still more broken in spirit. All these long to see their parents, if their parents still survive, to see their wives and children, to see their homeland, which they are naturally eager to revisit, especially since they will go back as great and rich men instead of insignificant and poor, with the treasures which they have gained from you.

'Do not now lead them on against their will. You will not find that they behave as they did in the face of danger now that their willingness for action has gone. You yourself, if you think it right, go home, visit your mother, take control of the affairs of Greece, take back to your father's house these many great victories. Then, if you wish, make a fresh start and organise another expedition against these same Indian tribes which live to the east, or if you prefer go to the Black Sea, or to Carthage and the area of Libya even further west. It is for you to decide. But other Macedonians and Greeks will follow you, young men instead of old, fresh men instead of exhausted veterans. To them the dangers of war hold no fear at present because they have not met them, and they will be eager for action in the hope of what they expect to achieve. They are likely to follow you still more keenly when they see those who first shared labour and danger with you returned to their families rich and famous, instead of poor and insignificant, as once they were. Above all, your majesty, it is a glorious thing to

75

show restraint at the time of success. As you command us and lead such an army as this there is no fear of any enemies. But the fate which comes to men from heaven is unexpected, and so you cannot guard against it.'

When Coenus finished this speech there was a burst of applause from the assembled company. Many even shed tears, showing still more their reluctance to face further dangers and their delight at the thought of returning home. But Alexander was angry that Coenus had spoken so freely and that the other officers were so reluctant to continue, and so he dismissed the meeting. On the next day he again angrily called together the same officers and said that he would himself go forward, but would not force any Macedonians to accompany him against their will. He would take men who would be glad to follow their king. Those who wanted to return home were welcome to do so, and could tell their friends that they had come back leaving their king in the midst of his enemies. So saying he went back to his tent, and for three days did not even allow any of the Companions into his presence. He was waiting to see if the Macedonians and their allies would have a change of heart, as often happens in a crowd of soldiers, and would become more easy to convince. But deep silence prevailed throughout the camp, and the men were clearly angry with his show of temper and were not changing their minds because of it. Ptolemaeus the son of Lagus records that he still made a sacrifice with a view to crossing the river, but the omens proved unfavourable. Then at last he called together the most senior of the Companions and in particular his closest friends, and said to the army that as everything indicated that they should withdraw he had decided to turn back.

There was a shout of joy such as a motley crowd of men would raise in their delight; most of them burst into tears. Some flocked to the king's tent, calling down blessings on Alexander because he had allowed himself to be defeated by them alone. Then he divided the army into detachments and gave orders for the building of twelve altars, as high as the highest towers and even wider than any normal tower. These were thank-offerings to the gods who had brought him so far victoriously, and also memorials of what he had achieved. When the altars were built he made a sacrifice on them in the proper manner, and held games involving athletes and horses. He set Porus to rule over the land up to the river Hyphasis, and he himself set off back towards the Hydraortes, which he crossed and then pressed on to the river Acesines. There

76

he found the city which he had previously ordered Hephaestion to build already completed. In it he settled any of the local inhabitants who volunteered, and those of his mercenaries who were no longer fit for service. He himself made his preparations for the voyage down river to the Indian Ocean.

6 Alexander's return to Babylon and death

If the troops thought that turning back signalled the end of their problems they were very much mistaken. Alexander may not have been able to extend his empire further, but he certainly intended to round-off what he had already gained. As we saw when Alexander addressed his officers at the river Hyphasis, he had geographical theories about communications between east and west. He was anxious to establish settlements, as he had done throughout his expedition, and to secure trade routes. Thus his return would be by a different route. But that would take him through different peoples, as yet unconquered, who were sure to resist a passing army which would try to steal their cattle and crops, as it had to do to survive. Before he had travelled far down the river Hydaspes Alexander was involved in war with the Malli, and here he suffered the most severe wound of his life. He had been wounded many times before, but never so seriously as this, and the story shows both his extraordinary daring, not to say rashness, in battle, and the deep devotion of his soldiers towards him.

On the next day Alexander divided his army and assaulted the Mallian city, taking personal command of one section while Perdiccas led the other. From the first the Indians did not face up to the Macedonian attack, but abandoned the city walls and fled to the citadel. Alexander and his force tore down a small gate and penetrated into the city ahead of the others. But Perdiccas' force fell behind as they had difficulty in crossing the walls. Most of them had not brought scaling ladders, because they thought that the city had been captured when they saw the walls abandoned by their defenders. When they saw that the citadel was still in enemy hands and that many soldiers were drawn up in front of it to defend it, some at once began to undermine the citadel wall, while others put up ladders wherever they could and tried to force their way in. But those Macedonians who were bringing the ladders seemed to be too slow for Alexander's liking, and so snatching a ladder from one of the men carrying it he himself put it up to the wall and began to climb, crouching under his shield. Behind him came Peucestas carrying the sacred shield, which

Alexander had taken from the temple of Athena at Troy and which was always carried before him in battle. After him was Leonnatus, an officer of the bodyguard, on the same ladder, while Abreas, one of the soldiers who had earned promotion to double pay, went up by a different ladder. The king was now up to the battlement on the wall, and leaning his shield against it he drove some of the Indians back, killed others there with his sword, and so cleared the wall of defenders at that point. The Guards, in terror for their king, rushed eagerly up by the same ladder, but broke it, so that those who were already climbing up were thrown down and the others had no way of getting up.

As Alexander stood on the wall he was shot at from the nearby towers all round, although none of the Indians dared to approach him. Those still resisting in the city also made him their target, aiming from close range as there was a piece of high ground near that part of the wall. It was quite clear that this was Alexander, both from the splendour of his armour and his remarkable courage. He at once realised that if he stayed there he would be in great danger and would achieve nothing worthwhile; but if he jumped down inside the wall he might perhaps in this way terrify the Indians, and if he did not achieve this, and had to face critical danger, he would not die without an effort, but would accomplish a great deed worthy to be told in future ages. With this in mind he leapt down from the wall into the citadel. Then, standing firmly by the wall, he laid about him with his sword and killed some of the Indians who came within striking distance, including their leader who rushed at him too rashly. Hurling stones also he checked another who approached, and then another, while anyone who came too close he cut down with his sword. But the natives were now reluctant to come within range, and standing back they bombarded him from all sides with any missiles that they happened to have or could find.

Meanwhile Peucestas, Abreas and Leonnatus, who alone had managed to get onto the wall before the ladders collapsed, also jumped down and joined the fight for their king. Abreas fell there, shot in the face by an arrow, and Alexander himself was hit, the arrow passing through his corselet into his chest at the top of the lung. Ptolemaeus says that air was breathed out of the wound along with the flow of blood. While the flowing blood was warm Alexander managed to defend himself although he was in pain. But when there was a greater flow of blood, as there was bound to be with breath also escaping there, he was overcome by dizziness and faintness, and he fell forward onto his shield. Peucestas stood over his fallen king and held over him the sacred shield from Troy, while Leonnatus stood beside him. These two were both now under fire, while Alexander was nearly unconscious from loss of blood.

The Macedonian attack had now become desperate. They had seen Alexander under fire on the wall and had seen him leap down into the citadel. In their eagerness, and in fear that the king might come to some harm from his thoughtless rashness, as the ladders were broken they had to contrive whatever means they could in this crisis to get onto the wall. Some drove pegs into the wall, which was made of clay, and hauled themselves up with difficulty by clinging to these, while others climbed up on each other's shoulders. The first up threw themselves over the wall, and then they saw the king lying there. All let out a cry of grief and anger. At once there was a violent struggle over the fallen king as one Macedonian after another held his shield over him. Meanwhile others had smashed the bar which secured the gate between the towers, and they were getting in in small groups. Others drove their shoulders at the gap in the gate, forced it inwards, and so opened the way to the citadel.

Now they began to slaughter the Indians, and they massacred them all, sparing neither woman nor child. Others carried away the king, lying on his shield in a critical condition, not sure whether he could possibly survive. Some say that Critodemus, a doctor from Cos, of the family of Asclepius, cut round the arrow and drew it from the wound. Others record that Perdiccas, one of the bodyguard, cut round the wound with his sword, on Alexander's order, as no doctor was present at the moment of crisis, and so removed the arrow. When it was pulled out there was a great rush of blood, so that Alexander fainted again, and so the bleeding was checked by his fainting.

> Arrian now digresses to discuss alternative versions of this story, that it happened at a different place, or that different people were involved.

While Alexander remained there and received treatment for his wound, the first news to reach his base camp for the Mallian expedition was that he had died from the wound. At once wailing swept through the whole army, as word spread from one to another. But when the first sorrow eased they were dismayed and in despair. Who would lead the army? For in Alexander's view and in the eyes of the Macedonians many seemed to be on an equal level of ability. How would they reach their homeland in safety? So many warlike tribes were all around them; some had not yet surrendered and were likely to fight fiercely for their independence, others were sure to rebel when their fear of Alexander was removed. They also believed they were surrounded by impassable rivers, and everything seemed hopeless and impossible to face without Alexander. But when news came that Alexander was alive they scarcely believed it, and they did not yet accept that he would recover. Even when a letter arrived from him saying that he would soon reach the camp most did not believe it because of their overwhelming fear, but they thought it had been forged by his bodyguards and senior officers.

When Alexander became aware of this he was afraid that the discipline of the army might break down, and as soon as he was able he was taken to the banks of the Hydraortes and sailed down stream. The camp was at the junction of the Hydraortes and Acesines, where Hephaestion was commanding the army and Nearchus the fleet. When the ship carrying the king was approaching the camp he ordered the awning to be taken from the stern, so that everyone could see him. They still disbelieved it, thinking that his dead body was being brought down stream, until, as the ship approached the bank, he raised his hand to the crowd. Then indeed they cheered, holding up their hands to heaven or reaching out towards Alexander. Many could not help shedding tears at the unexpectedness of it. Some of the Guards brought a stretcher for him as he was being lifted from the ship, but he told them to bring his horse. When he mounted the horse and could again be seen, the whole army broke into applause so loud that the banks and nearby woods re-echoed. When he reached his tent he dismounted from the horse and could be seen walking. Then they crowded all round him, some touching his hands, some his knees, some his clothes. Some simply stood near him and gazed, uttered a word of thankfulness and turned away. Others threw garlands and flowers such as grow in India at that time.

Nearchus records that some of Alexander's friends annoyed him because they criticised him for going ahead of his army at such personal risk. This, they said, was not the duty of a general but of an ordinary soldier. I think that Alexander was angry with what they said because he knew that they were right and that he deserved the criticism. Yet such passion always came over him in battle, and such was his love of glory, that just as other men are powerless to resist the pleasures that attract them, he had not had the strength of will to keep out of danger.

. . . .

In the southern reaches of the Indus Alexander's desire to explore and to open trade routes became most apparent. If his ideas were correct a sea route could be established from India to Asia, while he himself had declared that he expected his fleet to sail from the Persian Gulf via South Africa to Libya and the Pillars of Heracles (the Straits of Gibraltar) on the one hand, and that he expected the eastern sea to link up with the Hyrcanian Sea, i.e. the Caspian Sea, presumably by a northern route, on the other. One can only wonder what he would have made of his empire, in welding it together by trade routes and expanding man's knowledge of geography by further exploration, had he lived.

At Pattala the Indus divides into two great rivers, and both retain the name 'Indus' until they reach the sea. At the division Alexander began to build a harbour and dockyards. When the work had made some progress he decided to sail down the westerly river to its mouth. He sent Leonnatus with a thousand cavalry and about eight thousand of the heavy and light infantry to the island of Pattala, to keep company with the fleet. He himself took the fastest of his ships, the one-and-a-half bankers, all the thirty-oared ships and some of the light galleys, and sailed down the western river. But he had no pilot for the voyage, because the Indians in the area had fled, and so he found serious difficulties. On the day after they set off a storm broke, and as the wind was blowing against the current it caused steep troughs between the waves. The ships were severely shaken and most of them suffered damage; some of the thirty-oared ships became completely unseaworthy. However they managed to get to shore before they broke up, and there new ships were built.

Alexander then sent the most active of his light troops into the interior to catch some of the Indians, and these acted as pilots for the rest of the voyage. When they reached the point where the river opens out, so that at its broadest it is twenty-five miles wide, a strong wind was blowing in from the open sea. The oars could scarcely be lifted clear of the waves, but they ran for shelter to a side channel to which the pilots guided them. When they were anchored there a quite normal event occurred, the ebb tide, so that the ships were stranded on dry land. But Alexander's men had not known of this, and it caused them considerable dismay. They were even more surprised when, as time passed, the water flowed back in and the ships were re-floated. The ships which had settled squarely on the mud floated off again without damage and continued the voyage, as they had come to no harm. But those which had been stranded on a harder surface without an even support either collided with one another as the tide flooded in, or dashed against the hard bottom and were broken up. Alexander repaired these from what means he had, and sent two of the light galleys down stream to have a look at the island called Cilluta, where the natives said he should anchor on his voyage to the sea. They reported back that the island was large and had a good water supply, and that there was indeed an anchorage there, and so the rest of the fleet put in to it. But Alexander himself pressed on further with the best of his ships, to see where the river flowed into the sea and if the voyage out would be easy. After sailing about twenty-five miles down stream from the island they sighted another island out in the open sea. At that they returned to the island in the river, anchored at a headland, and Alexander offered a sacrifice to the gods which he said he had been told by Ammon to honour. On the following day he sailed to the island out at sea. Going ashore there also he made sacrifices, but to different gods and with different ceremony, which again he claimed were made in accordance with the oracle of Ammon. He then passed through the estuary of the Indus and sailed into the open sea, to find out, so he said, if there was any nearby country in the ocean. But I think his main reason was that he wanted to have sailed in the great ocean beyond India. He sacrificed bulls there to Poseidon and threw them into the sea, and after the sacrifice he poured a drink offering and threw the cup, which was of solid gold, and some golden bowls into the sea as thank-offerings. He prayed that Poseidon would allow a safe passage to the naval expedition which he intended to send with Nearchus to the Persian Gulf and to the mouths of the Euphrates and Tigris.

On his return to Pattala he found the citadel fortified and Peitho back with his army, after accomplishing everything which he had been told. Hephaestion was ordered to make the necessary preparations to fortify the harbour and build the dockyards. For Alexander intended to leave a considerable fleet at the city of Pattala where the Indus divides. He himself sailed down to the ocean again, this time by the other channel of the Indus, to find out which outlet of the Indus into the sea was safer. The two mouths of the river are about two hundred and twenty-five miles apart. On his voyage towards the river mouth he came to a great lake, created by the widening of the river and perhaps by other tributaries flowing into it. In fact it is very like a gulf of the sea. Species of fish normal in the open sea were found in it, and bigger than the ones in our waters. Alexander accordingly anchored in the lake where the pilots suggested, and left most of the soldiers and all the light galleys there with Leonnatus. He himself sailed beyond the river mouth with the thirty-oared ships and the one-and-a-half bankers, and so reached the open sea. He found that the voyage by this branch of the Indus was the easier. After anchoring off shore he took some cavalry with him and travelled for three days along the coast, to find out what the country was like past which the fleet must sail, and giving instructions for wells to be dug, so that the sailors could obtain water. He then returned to the ships and sailed back to Pattala, but he sent part of the army down to the coast to continue the same tasks, and with orders to return to Pattala when they had finished. He then sailed down stream again to the lake, and built another harbour and more dockyards. Leaving a garrison at that spot, he collected sufficient supplies to last the army for four months, and everything else needed for the coastal voyage.

. . . .

In the last months of 325 B.C. Alexander's army suffered its most severe losses in all the years of his leadership, not at the hands of an enemy but through the natural hazards of a desert. His purpose was to travel in conjunction with his fleet, probably with the ships carrying food for the soldiers, and the soldiers digging wells to provide water for the sailors. It would be the most obvious proof of the viability of the trade route which he hoped to open up. But the fleet was delayed by contrary winds and the army was left to fend for itself in conditions of appalling heat, with little food or water, in trackless desert. Modern travellers have thought it practically impossible for such an army to cross Gedrosia at all, but in fact they did. Alexander had miscalculated badly, probably believing that as nothing had proved impossible for him in the past nothing would be impossible in future. Stories of the journey tend to speak of his success in getting the army through. We may care to spare a thought for those who died so unnecessarily, certainly thousands of them, and wonder whether it was really a success.

From there he passed on through Gedrosian territory by a route which was difficult and offered no supplies. In particular there was no water for the army in many places. They were forced to make much of the journey at night, well inland from the sea, although Alexander himself was eager to pass along the coastal strip. He wanted to see what harbours there were, and to make whatever preparations were possible ready for the fleet, by digging wells or arranging an anchorage and a means to obtain stores. But the seaward area of Gedrosia was entirely desert. However Alexander sent Thoas, the son of Mandrodarus, to the sea with a few cavalry, to see if there happened to be an anchorage there, or any water and other provisions not too far away. On his return Thoas reported that he had found a few fishermen on the coast, living in stifling huts made by fixing shells together, and roofed with the backbones of fish. These men managed with little drinking water, scraping away the shingle with difficulty to get it, and then it was not always fresh.

When Alexander reached a part of Gedrosia where provisions were more abundant, he divided what he had obtained among the baggage trains, sealed it with his personal seal, and ordered it to be taken down to the sea. But while he was heading for the camping place where he would come nearest to the sea, the soldiers, including those detailed to guard the baggage, ignored the seal and made use of the provisions, and gave them especially to those who were suffering most from hunger. They were so overcome by their suffering that it seemed sensible to them, quite reasonably, to pay more attention to the death that was obviously threatening them than to worry about the uncertain and distant prospect of punishment from the king. When Alexander realised how necessary this had been he forgave what they had done. He then sent parties through the country and collected up what provisions he could for the army sailing with the fleet, and sent Cretheus of Callatis to deliver them. He also told the natives to bring as much ground corn as they could from the interior, dates from the palm trees, and sheep for the army to buy. He then sent Telephus, one of the Companions, to another place with a small supply of flour.

He himself pressed on towards the Gedrosian capital, Pura, which he reached after a journey from Oria of sixty days in all. Most of those who have told Alexander's story say that all that his army suffered in Asia was nothing compared with what they suffered here. Alexander did not go that way without realising the difficulty of the route (although only Nearchus says that he knew of the problems) but because he had heard that no one had yet made the journey successfully with an army, except when Semiramis fled from India, and the natives say that even she only got through with twenty survivors. Cyrus, the son of Cambyses, also made the journey, but with only seven survivors. For Cyrus had come into this area intending to invade India, but lost most of his army, because of the barrenness and difficulty of the route, before he could get there. These stories filled Alexander with a desire to surpass Cyrus and Semiramis. It was for these reasons, and also to be near enough to the fleet to provide it with stores, that Nearchus says Alexander went this way.

The blazing heat and lack of water destroyed most of the army, and especially the baggage animals. These died mostly from thirst, but also from the depth and heat of the scorching sand. They came across high hills of deep sand, not packed firm but letting them sink in when they trod on it, as if into mud or untrodden snow. Also both when going up and down hill the horses and mules suffered still more from the uneven and insecure surface of the road. The length of the stages was particularly unpleasant for the army. For water was not found regularly, and this compelled them to make marches as necessity demanded. When they covered the necessary distance at night and reached water in the morning they did not suffer too badly. But if they were still left marching as the day passed, because of the length of the stage, then they really suffered from the heat and in the grip of unquenchable thirst.

The loss of baggage animals was great, and the army was responsible for some of it. For when their provisions were short they got together and killed many of the horses and mules and ate their flesh, claiming that they had died of thirst or collapsed from exhaustion. Nor was anyone going to tell the truth about what they had done, because of their sufferings and because they were all doing the same thing. Alexander was not unaware of what was happening, but realised that to pretend not to know was a better way to deal with the situation than to let them see that he was accepting such indiscipline. A further problem was the difficulty of helping along those soldiers who were sick or who collapsed from exhaustion. They were short of animals to carry them, and the men themselves kept breaking up the carts, which could not be dragged along in the deep sand. In fact on the first stages they had been compelled for this reason to travel not by the shortest routes but by those which were easiest for the waggon teams.

So men were left behind on the roads, some sick, some overcome by exhaustion, heat or thirst. There was no one to help them along, nor men to stay and look after them. For the march was pushed on with the utmost speed, and in the concern for the army as a whole what happened to individuals was inevitably neglected. Some even fell asleep during the march, since much of the journey was made at night. When they woke up those who had the strength followed in the tracks of the army, but only a few from all that number reached safety. The majority fell and died on the sand, like men lost at sea.

Another disaster also struck the army, one of the worst to affect the men, horses and baggage animals. For just as in India, so too in Gedrosia there is much rain during the monsoon, not over the plains but over the hills, where the clouds are driven by the wind and pour out their rain when they cannot rise over the hilltops. The army had camped near a small stream, for the convenience of the water supply, but in the second watch of the night the stream which flowed there was swollen by the rain. The rain had fallen out of sight of the army, but it swept down the stream in such a flood that it drowned most of the women and children who were accompanying the army, and swept away the whole of the king's accommodation and the surviving baggage animals. The soldiers themselves only reached safety with the greatest difficulty, saving their weapons, but not always even those. Many also, when they drank, finding abundant water after the heat and thirst, died through drinking too much. For this reason Alexander usually pitched camp not right by the water, but up to two and a half miles away, so that they would not all rush into the water in a crowd and so cause the death of men and beasts. He was also afraid that those with least self-control would rush right into the springs or streams and pollute the water for the rest of the army.

At this point I am sure I must not overlook a particularly remarkable act on Alexander's part, whether it happened in this place or before that, among the Parapamisadae, as some writers have said. The army was marching across the sand in blazing heat, and they had to keep going until they reached water which was still far ahead. Alexander was also suffering from thirst, but he led the way on foot, great effort though it was. When they saw him sharing their hardship, the other soldiers bore their difficulties more easily, as usually happens in such circumstances. At that moment some of the light infantry, who had gone off from the rest of the army in search of water, found a meagre little trickle collected in a shallow gully. They collected it up with difficulty and hurried to Alexander as if they were taking him a great gift. When they approached they poured the water into a helmet and offered it to the king. He accepted it and thanked those who had brought it. But when he received it he poured it out on the ground for all to see. The whole army was so heartened by this act that you would have thought that the water which Alexander had poured away had provided a drink for every man. I praise this act of Alexander above all others, as a proof of his powers of endurance and of his inspiring leadership.

Another crisis also came upon the army in this area. For the guides finally had to admit that they no longer remembered the way. The landmarks had been obliterated as the wind blew the sand over them. Amid the endless sand, heaped up all alike, there was no way of distinguishing the route, not the usual trees growing along the road, nor any hill of firm earth rising up. The guides had not learnt to distinguish the way by the stars at night or the sun by day, as sailors do, the Phoenicians using the Little Bear and other sailors the Great Bear. Alexander however felt that they ought to head off to the left, and taking a few cavalry with him he went on ahead. As their horses grew exhausted from the heat he left most of them behind, and himself rode on with a total of five companions until he reached the sea. By digging away the shingle on the beach he found fresh, pure water, and soon the whole army arrived. For seven days they marched by the sea, obtaining water from the shore. Eventually the guides recognised the route and they again headed into the interior. When at last they reached the capital of Gedrosia the army was able to rest.

Alexander was now joined by the commander of his fleet, Nearchus, who had come inland to find him. Satisfied that all was well he sent Nearchus off to complete his voyage to the head of the Persian Gulf. He himself continued overland to Susa which he reached early in 324 B.C. On his way he restored the tomb of Cyrus, a former Persian king, which had been the target of vandalism. This was in part a symbolic act, as Alexander claimed to have taken over the throne and so to be himself a successor of Cyrus. It would also be a helpful means of encouraging the loyalty of his Persian subjects.

But all had not been well in his absence. In an empire of such a size a king ruled where his power could be felt. Alexander had been long gone; the danger from the enemy and the difficult country had encouraged some of his representatives in different parts of the empire to suppose that he would never return. Alexander now listened carefully to reports, deposed some of his officials, and executed others. A strong hand was at the centre of affairs again. At the same time, if the story is true, Alexander took two more wives, one the daughter of Darius. The problem of uniting the Macedonians and the Persians was central to any success in creating a truly united empire. He also added more natives to his army. Obviously the soldiers of Macedonia could not physically control such a wide area. Yet tensions were inevitable, as Arrian's account shows.

At Susa Alexander held wedding ceremonies for himself and the Companions. He himself married Barsine, the eldest daughter of Darius, and another wife as well, according to Aristoboulus, Parysatis the youngest daughter of Ochus. He was already married also to Roxane, the daughter of Oxyartes the Bactrian. He gave Drypetis, another daughter of Darius and so his own wife's sister, to Hephaestion, as he wanted Hephaestion's children to be his nephews. To Craterus he gave Amastrine, the daughter of Darius' brother Oxyartes, and to Perdiccas the daughter of Atropates the governor of Media. He gave to Ptolemaeus of the bodyguard and to his personal secretary Eumenes the daughters of Artabazus, Artacama and Artonis respectively. Nearchus married the daughter of Barsine and Mentor, Seleucus the daughter of Spitamenes the Bactrian, and similarly eighty other Companions married the noblest daughters of the Persians and Medes.

The weddings were conducted in Persian style. Chairs were set out for the bridegrooms, and when toasts had been drunk the brides came and sat beside their husbands, who took them by the hand and kissed them. The king set the example and all the weddings took place in the same way. This seemed to be a striking example of Alexander's fellowship with his people and his army. After the ceremony the husbands took their brides away, and Alexander gave wedding presents to them all. He also ordered all the Macedonians who had married Asian women to have their names officially recorded. There were over ten thousand of them, and Alexander gave wedding presents to them all.

Alexander also thought this a good opportunity to pay off the debts of the army, and he ordered a list to be made of what each man owed, on the understanding that they would receive the money. At first only a few entered their names, fearing that this was a test devised by Alexander to find out which soldiers had found their pay inadequate and had lived extravagantly. When Alexander discovered that the majority were not handing in their names, but were hiding any documents of debt which they had, he was angry at the suspicious attitude of the soldiers. He said that it was quite wrong for a king to do anything other than tell his subjects the truth, and equally wrong for the subjects to think that the king told anything but the truth. He then set up tables in the camp with money on them, and told the accountants responsible for it to pay off the debts of every man who produced a document of debt, without recording the names. So they realised that Alexander had told the truth, and the fact that he had not recorded their names pleased them even more than his payment of their debts. This gift to the army is said to have amounted to more than twenty thousand talents.

He also gave various gifts to other men, according to their reputation for general services, or if anyone had shown conspicuous courage in danger. He decorated with golden crowns men particularly noted for deeds of bravery, first Peucestas who had saved his life, then Leonnatus for doing the same, and for the dangers he had faced in India and his victory in Oria. For with the forces left to him he had faced the rebels of Oria and the neighbouring areas and had defeated them in battle, and had settled the general situation in Oria efficiently. Alexander also awarded a crown to Nearchus for his voyage along the ocean coast from India; for he had now arrived at Susa. Onesicritus, the helmsman of the king's ship, was similarly honoured, as were Hephaestion and the rest of the bodyguard.

The governors from the newly built cities, and from the rest of his conquered territories also came to him at Susa. They brought thirty thousand youths, all of the same age, whom Alexander called 'The Successors'. These were equipped with Macedonian weapons and trained for war in the Macedonian style. Their arrival is said to have offended the Macedonians, who thought that Alexander was doing everything he could to avoid having to depend on them in future. For the sight of Alexander's Persian form of dress had given no little irritation to the Macedonians, and the conducting of the marriages in the Persian style had not been to the liking of most of them, not even to some of those involved, although they were highly honoured in being put on terms of equality with their king. Peucestas, the governor of Persia, also provoked them by using Persian dress and language, while Alexander seemed to approve of his adoption of native habits. Some of the Bactrians, Sogdians, Arachotians, Zarangians, Areians, Parthyaeans, and those who are called

Euacae from Persia had been admitted into the Cavalry Companions, if they appeared to be men of merit and outstanding for their handsome appearance or some other quality. A fifth cavalry squadron had also been recruited, and although it did not consist entirely of foreigners, as the whole cavalry force was increased, some of the natives had been drafted into it. The following men had also been drafted into the Elite Corps – Cophen, the son of Artabazus, Hydarnes and Artiboles, sons of Mazaeus, Sisines and Phradasmenes, the sons of Phrataphernes who was governor of Parthyaea and Hyrcania, and Histanes, the son of Oxyartes and brother of Alexander's wife Roxane. Autobares and his brother Mithrobaeus were also included, and the commander appointed was Hystaspes the Bactrian. They were given Macedonian spears to replace their native javelins. All this offended the Macedonians, who thought that Alexander's outlook was becoming entirely oriental, and that he was regarding Macedonian customs and the Macedonians themselves without any respect.

.   .   .   .

From Susa Alexander's eagerness for further exploration took him up the Tigris. At this time he seems to have been very interested in developing water-borne communications in his empire, and it was indeed the quickest and best means of travel and trade in the ancient world. But at Opis the developing tension between Alexander and his Macedonians, jealous at the advancement of natives, came to a head.

When he reached Opis Alexander assembled the Macedonians and told them that he was discharging from the army all those who were unfit for fighting because of their age or permanent injuries, and he was sending them back to their own homes. On their departure he would give them gifts which would make them objects of envy to those at home, and which would rouse the other Macedonians to a desire to be involved in the same dangers and labours. Alexander certainly said this expecting to please them. But they were angry, not unreasonably, with what Alexander had said, for they thought he now despised them and regarded them as entirely useless for war. Throughout the whole of the campaign they had been provoked on many occasions. His Persian form of dress, indicating the same attitude, often annoyed them, as did his equipping the foreign 'Successors' in Macedonian style and his drafting of native cavalry into the ranks of the Companions. Therefore they did not take what he said quietly, but told him to discharge them all from the army and to carry on the campaign with his father – a scornful reference to Ammon.

When Alexander heard this he jumped down from the platform with his officers and ordered them to arrest those who were most openly stirring up the crowd. At that time he had become quicker-tempered, and he was no longer as well-disposed towards the Macedonians, as he had become used to oriental subservience. He himself pointed out to the Guards whom they should arrest. There were thirteen of them, and he ordered them to be taken away for execution. The rest fell silent in amazement, and he himself went back to the platform and made the following speech:

'I shall not make this speech, Macedonians, to check your desire to go home. You can go where you like, as far as I am concerned. But I want you to know as you leave how you have behaved towards me, and I towards you. I shall speak first of my father, Philip, as is only right. For Philip found you as poverty-stricken vagabonds, most of you dressed in skins, grazing a few sheep on the hills, and scarcely able to defend them against Illyrians, Triballians, and the nearby Thracians. He gave you cloaks to wear instead of skins, he brought you down from the hills into the plains, he made you worthy fighters, able to face the nearby foreigners, so that you could protect yourselves by your own courage and not by relying on your strongholds. He went on to make you city-dwellers, and he established civilised laws and customs. Instead of slaves and subjects he made you masters of those tribes by which previously you and your property used to be attacked and plundered. He added much of Thrace to the land of Macedonia, and by capturing the most suitable places on the coast he opened up trade for the country, and enabled you to work your mines without fear. He made you rulers over the Thessalians, before whom in the past you died of sheer fright, and when he humbled the Phocians he turned your way into Greece from a narrow and difficult track into a broad and easy road. The Athenians and Thebans had always been lying in wait to attack Macedonia. He brought them so low – and I was now sharing this work with him – that instead of our paying tribute to Athens and being subject to Thebes they in turn obtained their protection from us. He even advanced into the Peloponnese and settled affairs there. When he was appointed supreme commander of all the rest of Greece for the expedition against Persia he gained this honour not so much for himself as for the Macedonian people.

'These achievements of my father on your behalf are impressive in themselves, but trivial compared with my own. I inherited from my father a few gold and silver cups, and not as much as sixty talents in the treasury. I myself borrowed in addition eight hundred talents, and setting out from a country which did not even give you, its people, a good living, I at once opened up for you the straits of the Hellespont, although the Persians controlled the sea at that time. With my cavalry I defeated Darius' governors and added to your empire all Ionia and Aeolia, both Phrygias and Lydia, and I captured Miletus by siege. All the rest of Asia Minor came over to me voluntarily, and I gave it to you to reap the benefit. All the good things which I obtained from Egypt and Cyrene without striking a blow came to you. Lowland Syria, Palestine and Mesopotamia are your property; you possess Babylon, Bactria and Susa; the wealth of Lydia, the treasures of Persia, the good things of India, the outer ocean, all are yours. You are the governors, generals and captains.

'But what comes to me personally from these labours except the purple robe and this crown? I have taken nothing for myself, and no one can point out treasures belonging to me, separate from these possessions of yours and what is being kept safe for you. There is no reason why I should keep anything apart for myself. I eat the same food as you do and take the same sleep. And yet I do not think that I eat the same food as some of you, who enjoy luxurious meals, and I know that I wake before you so that you can sleep on.

'Perhaps you feel that while you were facing toils and hardships I myself gained these prizes as your leader without toil and hardship. But does any one of you feel that he has suffered more for me than I for him? Come along; if any of you has wounds strip and show them, and I will show you mine in return. No part of my body, at least in front, has escaped without a scar. There is not a weapon, whether used in hand-to-hand fighting or aimed at long range, of which I do not bear the marks on my body. I have been wounded by the sword, shot by arrows, hit by missiles from a catapult, often struck by stones and clubs, and all this for your sake, for your reputation, for your wealth. I am leading you in victory over every land and sea, across every river, mountain and plain. I married in the same way as you, and many of you will have children related to mine. Some of you had debts. I did not interfere to find out how they came about, when you were earning so much pay and taking so much plunder, whenever you had the chance of looting after a siege. I simply paid them off. Most of you have golden crowns as permanent records of your courage and my respect for you. When anyone has died his death has been glorious and his funeral splendid. Most of the dead have bronze statues at home; their parents are respected and have been released from all duties of service and taxation. For under my leadership not one of you has been killed because he turned his back.

'Now it is my intention to send away those of you who are unfit for further fighting, and to make you objects of envy to those at home. But since you all want to leave, be off all of you! And when you reach home tell them of your king, Alexander, who defeated the Persians, Medes, Bactrians and Sacaeans, who subdued the Uxians, Arachotaeans and Drangae, who gained control of the Parthyaeans, Chorasmians and Hyrcanians right up to the Caspian Sea. Tell them how he crossed the Caucasus beyond the Caspian Gates, crossed the rivers Oxus and Tanais, and the Indus as well, which no one but Dionysus had crossed before, and the Hydaspes, Acesines and Hydraortes, and would certainly have crossed the Hyphasis too, if you had not shrunk from it. Tell them how he reached the great sea by both mouths of the Indus, and how he crossed the Gedrosian Desert, where no one had ever been before with an army. Tell of his capture of Carmania as he passed by it, and of the land of the Oreitans, and how his fleet has completed the voyage from India to Persia. And then say how you brought him back to Susa and deserted him, going off and leaving him to the protection of the foreigners whom you have defeated. No doubt this news will win you honour from your fellow men, and will show the gods how dutiful you are! Away with you!'

As he finished Alexander jumped down quickly from the platform and went into the palace. He paid no attention to his bodily needs and did not even allow any of his friends to see him. Nor was he seen by anyone on the following day. On the third day he summoned to his presence picked men from the Persians, and divided among them command of the various units of the army. He now made it lawful only for those related to him to give him the customary kiss. But when the Macedonians had first heard his speech they had been shattered by what he said, and they remained in silence by the platform. No one followed the king when he rushed away, except his personal attendants and bodyguard. But the majority did not know what to do or say as they stood there, and yet did not want to go away. When they were told about the Persians and Medes, how high office was being given to Persians, foreign soldiers were being drafted into the units, a Persian force was being given a Macedonian name as the Elite Corps, Infantry Companions were being recruited from Persians and other nationalities, a Persian force of 'Silver Shields' was being formed, that there would be a Persian unit of Cavalry Companions, and a royal squadron at that, they could no longer control themselves. Rushing in a body to the palace they threw down their weapons before the door, as a sign of their humble pleading to the king. They stood in front of the door shouting and begging to be let in. They said they were willing to hand over those who had caused the recent disturbance and the outcry against the king, and they would not leave the door, day or night, until Alexander showed some pity on them.

When Alexander was told he came out eagerly, and as he saw their humble attitude and heard most of them shouting and wailing, he too shed tears. He stepped forward to address them, but they continued pleading with him. One of them, a man distinguished in the Cavalry Companions by age and rank, Callines by name, spoke first:

'Your majesty, what upsets the Macedonians is that you have made some of the Persians your relations; Persians are called relations of Alexander, Persians kiss you. But no Macedonian has yet tasted this honour.'

At once Alexander replied, 'Yet I regard all of you as my relations, and from this moment I shall call you so.'

At this Callines stepped forward and kissed him, and so did everyone else who wished. Then, picking up their weapons, they went back to camp cheering and singing their victory hymn. As a result of this incident Alexander made a sacrifice to the gods whom he usually honoured and held a public feast. He himself took his seat surrounded by all the Macedonians. Next to them came the Persians, and then the other nationalities who were distinguished in reputation or any other quality. The Greek priests and the Magi began the ceremony, and Alexander and those with him drew their wine from the same bowl and made the same drink offerings. Alexander prayed for many blessings, but especially for a friendly partnership in the empire between Macedonians and Persians. It is said that nine thousand people took part in the feast, and they all made the same drink offering and sang the same hymn.

After that those Macedonians who were unfit for war, because of their age or for any other reason, went away voluntarily. There were about ten thousand of them. Alexander gave them not only their pay for the time which they had served, but also for the time which the journey home would take. He also gave each man a talent over and above his pay. He told those who had children by Asian women to leave them with him. He did not want them to cause trouble in Macedonia between foreign children of foreign women and their own wives and children who had been left at home. He would see that these children were brought up in the Macedonian way, and in particular that they were trained for war. When they were grown up he would take them to Macedonia and hand them over to their fathers. These were the promises, vague and unsatisfactory as they were, which he made to the men as they left. But he thought it right to give a convincing proof of his affection and concern for them, and so he sent as their guardian and leader on the journey Craterus, his most loyal officer and a man whom he regarded as highly as himself. As he bade them farewell Alexander wept, and so did they all.

.   .   .   .

Alexander travelled on to Ecbatana and fought a winter campaign against nearby hill tribes, before returning to Babylon. He then began vigorous preparations for an expedition round Arabia. This was natural enough, as a continuation of the sea route he was developing, and linked with his theory that he could travel round his empire by sea and perhaps reach Gibraltar round the south coast of Africa. But it was hardly an attractive proposition to the troops with Gedrosia still fresh in their memory. What Alexander would have made of his empire we shall never know. Would the flow of conquest have continued, to take in Africa, the Mediterranean, Italy? Would he have succeeded in holding together such different peoples and governing them efficiently? Would he have created a united and prosperous world, built on his new trade routes and the chain of new towns and harbours, mostly called Alexandria, which marked the line of his passing? The world would surely have been a different place today if his dynamic character had been allowed thirty more years of achievement comparable with his first thirteen.

Alexander's death is something of a mystery. The course of his last illness is fully recorded, but some have found the detail suspicious. Was there someone anxious to produce ample evidence to show that the illness was natural and not the result of poison? The so-called Royal Diaries have been viewed with that suspicion. But obviously we can never possibly know. Certainly many may have welcomed his death, Macedonians jealous of his favour towards the

Persians, native officers seeking vengeance for their conquered country, ambitious men hoping to replace him, frightened men terrified of the dangers into which he might still lead them, some unsuspected person nursing a purely personal grievance. We have seen plots enough not to be surprised by another. It is amusing to speculate but quite pointless. It is sufficient to say that in his short lifetime Alexander had accomplished more than one has any right to dream of. His place as one of the greatest men in the history of the world is assured. We can leave the account of his death and the last word upon him to Arrian.

Alexander's death was now near. Aristoboulus records that the following incident occurred as a sign of what was to come. Alexander was drafting into the Macedonian units the troops which had come from Persia with Peucestas and from the coast with Philoxenus and Menander. But as he felt thirsty he got up from his place and left the royal throne empty. On each side of his throne there were couches with silver feet, on which his attendants had been sitting. Now some person of no consequence at all – some even say it was a man being held under open arrest – saw the empty throne and the couches, and the stewards standing near the throne. The king's attendants had left when he did, and so this man passed through the stewards and went up to the throne and sat on it. The stewards did not remove him from the throne, but because of some Persian custom tore their clothes and beat their breasts and faces as if some great disaster had happened. When Alexander was told he ordered the man who had sat there to be tortured. He wanted to know if he had done this as part of some plot. But the offender said nothing more than that it had suddenly occurred to him to do it. Accordingly the priests were even more convinced that what had happened meant no good.

A few days later Alexander had offered his usual sacrifice to the gods, in thanks for good fortune, and had made further offerings as a result of the priests' advice. He then joined a feast with his friends and went on drinking late into the night. He is also said to have given animals for the army to sacrifice, and to have distributed wine throughout the companies and sections. Some historians say that he wanted to leave the drinking party and go to bed, but that he met Medius, whom he regarded as the most reliable of his friends at that time, and that Medius asked him to join him for a drink, for it would be a pleasant party. This is also the version of the Royal Diaries, that after the first drinking bout he carried on drinking with Medius. Eventually he rose, washed and went to bed, but on the next day he dined with Medius again and once more drank late into the night. When he left the party he bathed, and after his bath he ate a little and went to sleep where he was, already suffering from a fever.

On the next day he was carried out on a stretcher to conduct the sacrifices, as was his daily custom, and after he had dealt with them he lay in the men's quarters until dark. Meanwhile he continued to give his officers their orders for the coming expedition and voyage. Those going on foot were to prepare to start three days later, while those who would sail with him would set out the day after that. From there he was taken to the river on his litter, and he sailed across in a boat to the park, where he again bathed and rested. On the following day he again bathed and made his usual sacrifices. He then went to his room and lay down, but continued talking to Medius. He also instructed his officers to report to him in the morning. After this he ate a light meal, but when he was taken back to his room he spent the whole night in a fever. On the next day he again bathed and sacrificed. He also gave instructions to Nearchus and the other officers for the conduct of the voyage in two days' time.

On the following day he bathed once more and made the regular sacrifices and fulfilled his religious duties, but had no relief from the fever. Even so he called in the officers and gave orders that preparations for the voyage should be completed. He bathed again in the evening but was now seriously ill. On the next day he was taken to the house near the bathing place. He made his usual sacrifices, and although he was so ill he still summoned the senior officers and gave further instructions for the voyage. A day later he was scarcely able to be taken out for the sacrifices, but he did conduct them, and still gave his officers more orders about their voyage. On the following day too, ill as he was, he still made his sacrifices. However he told the generals to wait in the courtyard, and the battalion and company commanders outside the door. He was now very ill indeed, and was taken back from the park to the palace. When the officers came in he recognised them but said nothing, and in fact his power of speech had gone. His fever remained severe all that night and day, and the next night and day as well.

This is the account given in the Royal Diaries. They also say that the soldiers were anxious to see him, some wanting to see him while he was still alive, others hearing a rumour that he was already dead and, I suppose, suspecting that his death was being concealed by his bodyguards. But most pushed their way in to see Alexander in grief and longing for their king. They say that he could not speak as the army filed past, but that he raised his hand, and with an effort raised his head and had a sign of recognition in his eyes for each man. The Royal Diaries say that Peithon, Attalus, Demophon, Peucestas, Cleomenes, Menidas and Seleucus spent the night in the temple of Serapis, and asked the god if it would be better for Alexander to be brought into the temple, and so to make his prayer and be cured by the god. But the word of the god was that he should not be brought into the temple, but that it would be better for him to stay where he was. The Companions published this reply, and not long afterwards Alexander died, for this was indeed the better thing which the god had meant.

Alexander died in the hundred and fourteenth Olympiad when Hegesias was archon at Athens [323 B.C.]. He lived for thirty-two years and eight months, as Aristoboulus records, and was king for twelve years and eight months. Physically he was very handsome, he had great endurance and a very alert mind. In courage, ambition and readiness to take risks he was outstanding, and he was very conscientious in religious matters. In physical pleasures he was very temperate, and glory was his only insatiable desire. He was remarkably quick to see what he had to do when the situation was obscure, and very skilful in guessing what was likely to happen from what he could see, while he was the complete master at organising, arming and equipping an army. He showed true nobility in raising the spirits of his soldiers, filling them with optimistic hopes, and driving away their fear in moments of danger by his own fearlessness. When he had to act in an unclear situation he did so with the greatest boldness. He was brilliant at seizing an advantage, moving before his enemy had any suspicion of what was going to happen. He was completely reliable at keeping promises and agreements, but never likely to be caught out by those who tried to deceive him. He was very careful about spending money on his own pleasures, but quite unstinting in benefiting his friends.

If Alexander made any mistake in haste or anger, or if he was led into behaving with foreign arrogance, I do not think it mattered. We must remember with sympathy Alexander's youth, his unbroken successes, and that men who associate with kings try to please them and not to do what is best for them, and so will always be harmful company. But I do know that thanks to his noble nature Alexander alone of the kings of the past regretted what he did wrong. The majority, if indeed they realise that they have done some wrong, think that they can conceal it by pretending it was actually a good deed. Of course they are wrong. I am sure that the only cure for a misdeed is to admit it and to show that one regrets it. Their wrongs will not be entirely intolerable to the victims if the offender admits that he was wrong, while there is good hope that he himself will not make a similar mistake in future if he is obviously sorry for his earlier mistakes.

I do not think that it was a particularly serious fault that Alexander claimed a god as his father. It was probably a device to gain greater dignity in the eyes of his subjects. I am sure that he was no less distinguished a king than Minos, Aeacus or Rhadamanthus, who were all regarded as sons of Zeus without the men of old thinking it arrogant in any way. Nor was he inferior to Theseus the son of Poseidon, or Ion the son of Apollo. As for his wearing of Persian dress, I am sure it was a matter of policy towards the foreigners, so that their king would not seem entirely alien to them, while in the eyes the Macedonians he was trying to show that he was turning away from Macedonian abruptness and pride. For the same reason I think he drafted the Persian 'Golden Apple' regiment into the Macedonian units and added their nobles to his Elite Corps. His drinking parties, as Aristoboulus records, were not prolonged for the sake of the wine, for Alexander was not a heavy drinker, but because he enjoyed his friends' company.

Whoever criticises Alexander must not do so merely by pointing out things which deserve criticism, but he should consider all of Alexander's career together. Similarly he should first realise what sort of a man he himself is and what luck he personally has enjoyed, and then consider Alexander, a man who reached the height of human achievement, the undisputed king of both continents, who spread his name over the whole world. Can a man who is himself a nonentity, busy with trivialities and not even successful in them, criticise Alexander? I myself am sure that there was no race of men, no city at that time, nor even a single individual, to whom Alexander's name was unknown. And so I cannot believe that a man who was beyond comparison with any other was born without divine influence. Oracles are said to have indicated the same thing at Alexander's death, while various people are said to have had a variety of visions and dreams. The honour he still receives from men, and the memory of him, stronger than that of any normal man, suggests the same, and even now after so long a time other oracles given to the Macedonian people add to his glory. Although there are some things which Alexander did that I personally have criticised in my story, I am not ashamed to admit complete admiration for Alexander himself. When I had fault to find it was to uphold truth as I saw it and to benefit other men. That was why I undertook to write this book, and I am sure that I did not lack the help of god.

Index of translated extracts from Arrian's Anabasis of Alexander

Suggested books for further reading

Translated original sources
Arrian, *The Campaigns of Alexander*, translated by A. de Selincourt and J.R. Hamilton (Penguin)
Plutarch, *The Age of Alexander*, translated by I. Scott-Kilvert (Penguin)
Quintus Curtius, *History of Alexander* (2 vols.), translated by J.C. Rolfe (Heinemann, Loeb Classical Library)

Modern historical works
Robin Lane Fox, *Alexander the Great* (Allen Lane/Omega Books)
J.F.C. Fuller, *The Generalship of Alexander the Great* (Eyre and Spottiswoode)
J.R. Hamilton, *Alexander the Great* (Hutchinson University Library)
N.G.L. Hammond, *A History of Greece to 322 B.C.* (Oxford University Press)
W.W. Tarn, *Alexander the Great* (2 vols.) (Cambridge University Press)

Historical novels
Mary Renault, *Fire From Heaven* (Longman/Penguin)
Mary Renault, *The Persian Boy* (Longman/Penguin)

Index